BREAD *Afresh* WINE *Anew*

BREAD Afresh WINE Anew

Sermons by Disciples Women

Edited by
Joan Campbell
and David Polk

Chalice Press
St. Louis, Missouri

Library of Congress Cataloging–in–Publication Data

      Bread afresh, wine anew : sermons by Disciples women / edited by Joan B. Campbell and David P. Polk.
1. Christian Church (Disciples of Christ)–Sermons, American.
  I. Campbell, Joan B. II. Polk, David Patrick.
BX7327.A1B69 1991   252'.0663   91-29236
ISBN 0-8272-0218-0

Printed in the United States of America

Contents

Introduction   vii

What Is the Right Distance from the Pulpit to the Pew?   *Holly McKissick*   1

Singing the Lord's Song in a Strange Land   *Claudia Highbaugh*   7

Hold on for Your Blessing   *L. Susan May*   12

In the Middle of the Wilderness   *Sandra M. Messick*   17

Bearing the Burden   *Mary Donovan Turner*   21

For Such a Time as This   *Nancy Claire Pittman*   25

Prophetic Patience   *Stephanie Paulsell*   31

Strange Messengers   *Karen Leigh Stroup*   36

Soil and Water   *Charlotte Nabors*   42

Woman Preacher   *Connie Erickson*   47

Meticulous Mercy Is the Work of Travelers   *Rita Nakashima Brock*   52

Do You Want to Be Healed?   *Carolyn Bullard-Zerweck*   61

The Transfiguration   *Becky A. Hebert*   67

Why Are You Afraid?   *Diane Caughron*   72

Not Nut'n Not Nobody Not No How
   Amanda J. Burr   77

God Hears Our Tears   *Janet Hellner-Burris*   81

Can You Stand the Rain?   *Cynthia L. Hale*   86

Fools for Christ   *Kelly Boyte Peters*   91

The Art of Making Bread   *Beverly Dale*   95

We Know the Words—We Need Lives to Match!
   Mary Louise Rowand   99

Haunted   *Rebecca Z. Brown*   106

"Yes, Lord!"   *Lydia Land*   110

Eyes to See   *Eleanor Scott Myers*   113

Blinded by a Log   *Marsha Bishop*   117

Giving Birth to Compassion   *Marilyn W. Spry*   123

The Simple Covenant   *M. Margaret Harrison*   128

Real Humility, Real Faithfulness, Real
   Stewardship   *LaTaunya M. Bynum*   132

Bridges to Life   *Allene M. Parker*   137

One Flock, One Shepherd   *Joan B. Campbell*   144

In Search of a Blessing   *Jane McAvoy*   151

Embracing Sick Foreigners (Without
   Condescension)   *Drea Walker*   155

On the Edges of Terror/On the Edges of Hope
   Ola Irene Harrison   161

*I*ntroduction

Believe it or not, one can truly claim that the first person to preach the Christian gospel was a woman!

Her sermon was not very long. It takes only one verse of scripture, in John's Gospel, to record it. Mary Magdalene rushed back to the disillusioned disciples after her Easter encounter and announced the good news: "I have seen the Lord" (John 20:18). Luke's account identifies other women who also shared in the preaching, and appends a comment that their words struck the male disciples' ears as "an idle tale" (Luke 24:11). They refused to believe, until they had gone and seen for themselves.

Twenty centuries have come and nearly gone, and at last the idle tales are being heard more widely these days and received more appreciatively. The Holy Spirit has never favored gender discrimination, and pulpit committees are finally getting the message, albeit more slowly than many of us would hope. Some of the best preaching in Disciples pulpits these days is coming from those weavers of "idle tales."

This is a book of sermons by women. They are pastors, co-pastors, associate pastors, campus ministers, regional and general staff, doctoral students, college and seminary professors, and an ecumenical executive and a seminary president. Thirty-two proclamations of the good news appear on these pages, and they are as varied as the persons who delivered them. They have one thing very much in common: They bring fresh perspective to bear on an old familiar story.

Twenty-two years ago, the Disciples' publishing house produced a volume of sermons entitled *The Vital Pulpit of the Christian Church,* the third in a semicentennial series dating back to 1868. It shared with its predecessors one pivotal flaw. Even though women were being ordained to Christian ministry ever since Clara Hale Babcock in 1888, all twenty-eight sermons selected for the book were by men.

The vitality of Disciples pulpits is greatly enriched these days by the preaching of women. *Bread Afresh, Wine Anew* attempts to represent that richness. The selection process remained as free of prejudgments as possible. No conditions were imposed, no boundaries were set beforehand. Disciples women were invited to submit one or two of their best or favorite or most typical sermons. The structure and content of the book have emerged out of the reviewing and sifting of nearly one hundred sermon manuscripts submitted by fifty-five women.

Some patterns are discernible. Experiential preaching is certainly at the center of these messages, often vividly so. That is not unique to female preachers, of course, but it calls attention to an important aspect of Christian proclamation. The gospel is always being filtered through human experience that is culturally and historically conditioned. What we are able to see depends on where we're looking from and who is doing the looking. Our insight into the enduring good news is significantly expanded when we are exposed to witnesses whose voices have all too often been stifled or relegated to the kitchen. Their stories enhance our understanding of our stories, and ancient truths burst into our consciousness with exciting freshness.

There is an order and a flow that underlies the sequence of sermons on these pages, but it remains a subtle one. We leave it to the reader to determine the nature of it.

The editors are indebted to LaTaunya Bynum, Joey Jeter, and Daisy Machado for sharing with us the arduous task of evaluating the sizable amount of material that we received. But we accept full responsibility for the final decisions. To those sisters not included here, and to all whose lives are touched by these sermons, we express our hope that this collection represents a solid step forward toward gender equality in Christian pulpits everywhere.

Joan Campbell
David Polk

*W*hat is the right distance from the pulpit to the pew?

Holly McKissick

Holly McKissick is pastor developer of Saint Andrew Christian Church, Olathe, Kansas. A graduate of Brite Divinity School, she is a member of the General Board and Administrative Committee of the Christian Church (Disciples of Christ) and is active in peace and justice concerns. This sermon was preached at the Ministers' Institute of the Mid-America Region.

Genesis 19

A few words. That's all we have about Lot's wife. From the Hebrew, the text of Genesis 19:26 literally reads, "His wife looked behind him, and she thereupon turned into a pillar of salt." Just a few words: no detailed description, no character study, just one sentence.

But where scripture has been silent, tradition has not. In *All of the Women of the Bible,* Edith Deen reflects the well-developed tradition that has grown up around Lot's wife in these words: "[She] was a woman who ate and drank and lived for the things of the world...a worldly selfish woman, one who spent lavishly and entertained elaborately."[1] For centuries, Lot's wife—who is not even given a name—has served loyally as the greedy, wicked woman, stupid and self-serving. But her day may yet come. For here and there, Lot's wife is making a comeback—popping up in poetry, in literature, in modern midrash inspired by women rabbis or imaginative poets. It suggests that maybe her story has yet to be heard.

Celia Gilbert, in her poem "Lot's Wife,"[2] offers a sympathetic portrayal of a woman busy with domestic tasks and friendly with the women and children of the neighborhood. Gilbert goes on to weave her poem from Sodom and Gomorrah

1

to Hiroshima and Nagasaki. As she writes of the devastated cities, she paints a portrait not of a wicked shrew but of a decent, caring woman who cannot turn her back on her people, her community, her sisters and brothers, her friends, and her enemies. Lot's wife is connected to these people, bound to them through the ordinary—the daily rituals of washing and cooking, cleaning and gathering. Here we find one who cannot turn from the people because she is so related to the people, so close to their pain and fears, their hopes and dreams. Here we have the model of vulnerability. Left behind as a pillar of salt, she is the very embodiment of the people's struggle, a memorial to those who could not flee.

If we want to push our imaginations still further, Lot and Lot's wife could offer us two different models of ministry. One, represented by Lot, stands opposite the people, guiding, giving directions, offering wise counsel, making decisions, welcoming the people in—but never getting too close, and always comfortable with control and power. The other model, represented by Lot's wife, stands with the people, living, breathing, working among them, feeling what they feel, embodying their experience—to the point where there are few boundaries. Interdependence, but bordering perhaps on codependence.

My hunch is that in our ministry most of us move back and forth from Lot to Lot's wife, from detachment to overinvolvement. But my experience has been that in the area of worship, we err on the side of Lot, the side of detachment. We are at times so controlled, so held together, so on stage, that our vulnerability is hidden. We embody not the fragility of the human spirit, not the innocence of grace, not the humanness that we live and breathe, but too often distance—stifled and protected. And so our worship is not renewing. It is on the surface, superficial, even desperate at times. For real pain is not allowed, real confession is not spoken, true grace is not risked or believed.

When I was in college, I dated a young man whose father was a minister. I remember that sometimes after a prayer or a sermon, the young man would whisper to me, "That's not his real voice." Sometimes he would even say, "That's not really him at all." By our very human nature, we seek a place that feels safe, secure, protected. And yet ministry offers so little protection from the rough edges of life—death, cancer, divorce, depression. There are few places that are safe and secure. And so we are not always "who we are." We have a preacher's voice that we put on, a posture of control that we assume.

In the movie *Born on the Fourth of July*, there is a scene where a young soldier is confessing to his superior that in the confusion of the fire and shooting, he killed one of his fellow soldiers. The officer cannot hear the confession and insists that the young soldier did not kill his comrade. The young soldier continues to confess, and the officer says over and over, "No, I do not think you killed him. No, I am sure you did not. No, I know you did not. No, you did not...." The movie is full of painful scenes, but this one stands out: the young soldier, so full of terror and fear and guilt and shame, and the officer, so full of control and power and denial, so unable to hear the confession and acknowledge the pain of the situation, so unable to let the horridness of the war penetrate his being. "No, I do not think you killed him. No, I am sure you did not. No, I know you did not. No, you did not...."

Clinically speaking, we call this "denial." But it hits me somehow differently than denial—more like a pitiful attempt to be in control, to act as if things are all right when everyone knows things are not all right. The officer could not hear the confession. He had such a need to be in control, to be in power, to act as though there was reason behind a war when there was not, to pretend that progress was being made when more dead were being counted each day. He could not hear the confession, his face so rigid and tight, his body drawn up straight and unbending.

Just for a moment, I want us to think intentionally about the role of our own bodies—or as James Nelson would say, our "body-selves"—in the renewal of worship. What we look like. What we feel like. Think of a typical Sunday morning. Picture yourself preaching, praying, calling the people together. Where are you standing? What do you look like? How much of you is showing? Can the people see you or are you behind a lectern or table? Can you see the people? How close to the people do you get? Close enough to hear the confessions, the prayers, the songs of praise? Can they hear your confessions, your prayers, your songs of praise? Are you wearing a robe or a favorite suit? Do you sit in a pew or in a chair? Is it comfortable or awkward?

I have thought about these questions quite a bit lately because I am getting a new robe. I hope it gets here by Easter. I am getting a new robe because I finally decided I was either getting a new robe or leaving the ministry. The robe I have now doesn't fit. It never has. I remember when I ordered it during my last semester in seminary. My best friend and I walked over to the Cokesbury store to be sized for our robes. They didn't have any robes that fit. But they said, "Oh, don't worry, they're all custom made."

Well, I am getting a new robe because my so-called "custom-made robe" fits just about everyone I know except me. It fits my husband better than it fits me. Bo Jackson got married in the church I serve and I do recall that it was too small for his uncle, a small-town preacher who showed up without any clerical garb. But then I think bigness runs in the Jackson family.

I am getting a new robe because mine covers too much. I first realized that the robe hid who I was when I would visit people in the hospitals and they never recognized me without the robe on. "Are you that person on Sunday morning with the Texas accent?" "That's not you down there in the front, is it?" People who came every week, who shook my hand every week, who heard me pray ever week, said to me, "You must be new. When did you start?"

I am getting a new robe because mine covers too much: my humanness, my realness, my vulnerability. I am getting a new robe because I am not an angel or a spirit but flesh and blood, connected with people, knowing people, sensing people, loving people only through this body in which I live. I am getting a new robe because I want to be with the people, not separated from them or hidden from them.

But even this can be carried too far. Our openness, our care, our concern for others can be carried too far. Remember Lot's wife: She was so close to the people, so unable to separate herself from them, that in the end it destroyed her. In *Hopeful Imagination*, Walter Brueggemann writes, "A ministry of vitality requires that we be deeply concerned for and utterly free from other people." He continues, "We incline in think these are mutually exclusive postures, but it is the capacity to practice both that gives us energy for vocation."[3]

Deeply concerned for—and utterly free from. Somewhere in that tension is the energy for vital, renewed ministry and worship. When we are deeply concerned for people, we are vulnerable to them and before them. They affect us, we are related to them. So worship is never too rehearsed or stifled, but always connected with the people's hunger and thirst for grace. When we are utterly free from people, then we are empowered to preach from our hearts the word that has been given to us without fear of sanction or reprisal. The gospel cannot be co-opted and the prophetic voice finds strength and courage. Deeply concerned for, utterly free from.

Somewhere between Lot and Lot's wife is the place where the two are held together—the right balance, the place where we are close enough to hear the confession and yet still able to speak the word of grace.

In Genesis 2:25 we read that the man and the woman were naked and they were not ashamed. Now there is a difference between a robe that fits and appearing in the buff. There is a difference between sharing one's humanness and making one's personal struggle the center of every worship service. They were naked and not ashamed. The Hebrew can be translated, "They were vulnerable and it felt appropriate." Maybe that is what we are after: some way to lead worship where we are appropriately vulnerable, where worship is not too much cover-up or too much confession, not too much protection or too much self-proclamation.

Debra Peavey, a Disciples pastor in the Northwest, served the church for five years before coming out as a lesbian. The church weathered that struggle. I heard her speak this summer and she said that as she came out of the closet, others did too. They came out as people struggling with addictive behaviors— with alcohol, with physical abuse, with depression. Her vulnerability gave others permission to share where they were vulnerable. The congregation found a level of sharing that was appropriate for them. She said now they have come to understand that the church is a place where we tell the truth about who we are, where our weaknesses are shared and our vulnerability is appropriately respected.

Somewhere between Lot and Lot's wife is the place where we tell the truth about who we are: people in need of God's grace. It is the place where worship is renewing because everyone is given the grace to share openly their confessions and prayers, their joys and delights. Somewhere between Lot and Lot's wife is the place where worship is renewing because the need for grace and the presence of grace is embodied in the very one leading worship.

Picture yourself on Sunday morning. How much of you shows? It may be a great sermon or just the final product of a long, busy week, but how much of you shows? It may be a prayer that dances on your lips or comes only after much hesitation and halting, but how much of you shows? Does it show that you are standing there—whether trembling or self-assured—only by the grace of God? Can the people see you clearly, so there is no mistake that it is only the grace of God that sustains you for one more week? The benediction may come after a new family joins or on a rainy Sunday with a disappointing turnout, but can the people see the benediction—the "good word"—the word of grace embodied in the very one leading worship? Can they see it? Can they?

By God's grace, let it be so. Amen.

———

[1]Edith Deen, *All of the Women of the Bible*. Harper & Brothers, 1955, p. 17.

[2]Celia Gilbert, *Bonfire*. Alicejamesbooks, 1983.

[3]Walter Brueggeman, *Hopeful Imagination: Prophetic Voices in Exile*. Augsburg Fortress Press, 1986, p. 51.

Singing the Lord's song in a strange land

Claudia Highbaugh

Claudia Ann Highbaugh is associate university chaplain at Yale University. A graduate of Hiram College, she holds M.Div. and Doctor of Ministry degrees from the School of Theology at Claremont. Claudia is currently co-chair of the Caucus for Disciple Women Clergy.

Psalm 137:4

It is a very good thing I was asked to speak and not sing.
 I'm not Leontyne Price,
  no melodies like Johnny Mathis...
 Why, I couldn't carry a tune if it had a handle on it...
  I just don't sing!
It's a good thing,
 a very good thing,
  they asked me to *speak!*
And a good theme too!
I know an awful lot about "a strange land."
 The place I don't know,
   don't feel,
   can't find, is that
    promised land...
But I know about the "strange land."
It's a good thing they asked me to speak about my homeland.
 Just *seems* like I've always only known
  the Lord's song as my national anthem...
In every place I've known the Lord to be,
it was a strange land...to me!

7

The first place that God sang music to me, I was just a child.
Amidst the silent, solemn worship of squirming, scratching,
        always hungry children
        in the grade school Mass of my
        Episcopalian parochial education,
I heard loud and clear, a voice call me into God's world,
to serve...
        But when I looked around, only
        men and boys were there...
        dressed in robes, with candles, crosses, incense.
No female presence!

Must have been a wrong number, that call, or else
        the *very long* distance wires got crossed.
If memory serves me well,
I know the day the "strange land" became my home...
        That day in high school, a place
        of academic *fury*,
                power,
                pressure
                even fear.
A youth afraid of failure among the nation community of
God's own celebrated people, I turned that day to my advisor,
Mrs. Abatso, for help and comfort:
        "What of my future?" I said to her. "How will I fare,
        a poor ineloquent child of little accomplishment,
        How will I survive in the world of higher education?"
            "You won't," said she.
                "No smarts!
        You don't have the gifts of intellect,
            no originality, why even with this
            fine preparation, you must choose
            a school of your own people
            where students are slow, and labor,
            and do not require excellence, only
                    survival."

That day, I became a stranger, and knew from there,
        no song but God's own.
My own people would *not* have me excel, but only survive...
My God, from then, alone became and is my guide,
most days my only friend who understands
        the places I've struggled to be heard,

the history I've prayed to comprehend,
the theology I've cried over because their God,
    in German,
      does not either know or remember me.

My God, when will it end,
    this sojourn in too many foreign lifetimes?
Will it end in a small town in Kansas where sight unseen a
white man told his fear of me because I was black, a woman,
and ordained?
    No. Not here.
Will my visit to the strange land end in Texas, where
NIGGER is a public song screamed as a reminder by a caring
passerby?
    I fear not...
When will my strange land sojourn end? In California, where
everyone is strange? Perhaps my parishioners will call me
friend?
    No. It is not so,
    or safe to share the journey of a left-handed woman.
        She rants and raves.
      We'll let her in, but call her friend?
          Not yet...
And so it goes to journey's end, I suppose...

When will it end? Alone, alive, singing with no song...
    God's promise in any land is strange to me.
Perhaps my only hope is to know the lyrics soooo well, that
    speaking them,
      living them,
        hearing them, is melody enough...

"Do not press me to leave you
    or to turn back from following you!
Where you go, I will go;
    where you lodge, I will lodge;
your people shall be my people,
    and your God my God" (Ruth 1:16–17).

"Then I heard the voice of the Lord saying,
    'Whom shall I send, and who will go for us?'
And I said, 'Here am I, send me!'" (Isaiah 6:8).

And *what* does the Lord require of me?
   "To do justice, and to love kindness,
      and to walk humbly with your God" (Micah 6:8b).

"Watch for the opportune time, and beware of evil,
      and do not be ashamed to be yourself.
For there is a shame that leads to sin,
      and there is a shame that is glory and favor.
Do not show partiality, to your own harm,
      or deference, to your downfall.
Do not refrain from speaking at the proper moment,
      and do not hide your wisdom.
For wisdom becomes known through speech,
      and education through the words of the tongue.
Never speak against the truth,
      but be ashamed of your ignorance.
Do not be ashamed to confess your sins,
      and do not try to stop the current of a river.
Do not subject yourself to a fool,
      or show partiality to a ruler.
Fight to the death for truth,
      and the Lord God will fight for you."
                        (Ecclesiasticus 4:20–28)

    "Ask, and it will be given you; search, and you will find; knock, and the door will be opened for you. For everyone who asks receives, and everyone who searches finds, and for everyone who knocks, the door will be opened" (Matthew 7:7).

There came a woman of color to the door of God's Kingdom.
Jesus said to her, "Give me your life."
        "How is it you, one of God's chosen,
        ask me, a woman of color, to
        share in the Gospel of your life,
        me...a stranger who cannot sing?"
Jesus said, "You have the gift of life and the blessings of faith. Draw the song from the wellsprings of your experience and our lives will be entwined as a gift of song amidst the journey of life."

And so my journey from strange land to strange land,
      always a stranger,
      continues.

And I continue to sing God's song:
> like my sister Ruth, making a new way of God's way...
> like my sister Carla, speaking a foreign tongue...
> with my brother Eric, seeking a different vision...
> for my brother David, drawing deeply, from the
>   wellsprings of the Spirit...
> singing God's song in a strange land in my search for a
>   homeland.

God's call to all faithful folk is to step beyond comfort into calling.

"Singing God's Song" is to know the lyrics,
> speaking them,
>   loving them,
>   learning so well
that being a stranger is comfort enough.

> I
> am a black woman
> tall as a cypress
> strong
> beyond all definition still
> defying place
> and time
> and circumstance
>   assailed
>   impervious
>   indestructible
> Look
>   on me and be
> renewed[1]

---

[1] Mari Evans, *I Am a Black Woman*, William Morrow and Company, 1970, p. 12. Copyright © Mari Evans; reprinted by permission.

$\mathcal{H}$old on for your blessing

L. Susan May

Susan May is presently working on a doctorate in homiletics and ethics at Vanderbilt University. A graduate of Purdue University and Christian Theological Seminary, Susan served as associate minister of First Christian Church in Vincennes, Indiana, where this sermon was preached.

Genesis 32:22–32

Do you ever look at someone else's life and see an endless string of crises and tragedies and obstacles, and wonder to yourself, "How does this person make it?" Some people just seem as if they go through more than a human heart could bear, and they do it without giving up, or giving in, or losing heart. It's like that spiritual, "Nobody knows the trouble I've seen." And you wonder how they make it through their troubles without falling apart.

Sometimes, they may tell a friend, they may go to their pastor, or they may start seeing a therapist. Most likely they will see a therapist, on the assumption that their "coping" problem is not spiritual but psychological—a matter of the mind and not the spirit. But think again, because psychiatrists and psychologists tell us that most people come to them for a blessing, to be valued as individuals, to be encouraged, to be forgiven for the mess they have made of their lives.

Now, let's imagine for a minute that we have Jacob's family in for some family counseling. Wouldn't that give the therapist a shock? We have Mom and Dad and the twins, Jacob and Esau. Jacob, of course, is wearing that fake fur on his arms like in the Sunday school leaflets, to try to trick the therapist into getting

12

him confused with Esau, because Esau is Daddy's favorite. Jacob is Mommy's favorite. This is a family story of some serious sibling rivalry, parental conniving, trickery, and thievery. We know that before this is over, Jacob will not only steal the birthright and blessing from Esau, but he too will be tricked by his uncle Laban into marrying the wrong girl. If this were a TV show, it would be more like the family in "Dallas" than the family in "The Cosby Show," and Jacob would be J.R.

In today's episode, we find Jacob on the way back home to make up with Esau. Scared that Esau won't feel forgiving, Jacob's going to give him a few hundred goats, lambs, and cows—but he's not sure that livestock can make up for all his orneriness. Jacob is alone on one side of the river, with the wives and kids and cows on the other side for safekeeping against cattle rustlers.

This is some biblical hero, isn't it? Inside of Jacob is every brother or sister who's ever been jealous of the older/prettier/smarter one. Inside of Jacob is every big and little cheater, from the income tax fudger to the multimillion-dollar embezzler. Inside of Jacob is every person who's ever felt like a failure, everyone who's ever been disappointed in love. "Oh, Lord, look what's happened, I've got the wrong woman." Inside of Jacob is each and every one of us who has made some kind of mess out of life, or is trying to make life out of a mess. The widow who returns home after the funeral and buries her face in his bathrobe still hanging on the bathroom door. "Oh, God, I'll never make it." The young girl who discovers she's pregnant. The young man who feels pessimistic and discouraged that his life and goals don't count for much in the world. The old man who looks through the photo album and regrets missing the kids' childhood as they grew up. The stern-lipped couple dividing up furniture and weekends with the kids. Every unfaithful wife or husband.

All of us are like Jacob, hoping that God can't really see us, can't really see the deep inner life, the frustrations, temptations, and failures. Or maybe we feel more like Robin, a neighbor of mine in Indianapolis, who kept giving me feeble excuses for not visiting church with me. Finally, she said, "Susan, I'm not good enough to come to church. The baby's father and I...well, we're not married...and I just couldn't show my face inside a church." She needed a blessing.

"Jacob was left alone; and a man wrestled with him until daybreak." That's a long time to wrestle. I know that it wears me out to wrestle with a feisty six-year-old for more than five minutes. But the two wrestled—sweaty, I imagine; dirt and dust and sticks clinging to their arms and legs. And neither one of them would give up. Jacob would not let go until he got his blessing—locked together in face-to-face conflict with God or at least a divine messenger who, by any worldly kind of justice, should have just crushed him on the spot, given the kind of awful sinner that he was.

And guess what! We can struggle and not be defeated, we can struggle and survive, we can struggle and still get a blessing. The faithful life is not a life where there is no struggle, where there is no sin, where there is not heartache and disaster. The faithful life is the life where you have the courage to struggle alongside of God, with God, and to realize that God neither crushes you, nor is crushed.

Through the struggle comes the blessing, the new name, the new identity in God. Somehow, through all your struggles, you discover that God is right there with you, that God is not the one who curses you or crushes you, but God is the one who strives with you and blesses you. Accepts you. Loves you in spite of the fact that you are only able to do a little bit of good a little bit of the time.

Hold on for your blessing. When things seem impossible, be sure that God will get you through it—and, like Jacob, know that God will love and care for you, and struggle with you, and bless you no matter what, so that you can get on with the business of living. You can go on and do things according to God's ways, you can hold onto God for your blessing and not have to depend on the world to bless you.

Hold onto God. Hold onto the God of love and forgiveness that you meet face to face in Jesus Christ. This is the kind of God we hold onto. Not a tyrant God, not an indifferent God who put the world together and sits on the sidelines watching while we fumble around on the playing field. God is right in there with us, sweaty, dirty, reliable, and ready to keep on blessing and loving us in spite of our poor plays and feeble players.

And it worked! Amazing, ruthless grace worked on Jacob. He made up with his brother, Esau, and went on to become the father of Israel. He may have come away limping, but we all limp through our faith lives; none of us is equal to the task. And sometimes we cannot get through the struggles of faith without some broken legs, broken dreams, broken hearts. But we keep on anyway. We hold on for the blessing that comes from knowing that we have done the best that we could at a particular time, and that we have helped advance the Kingdom just a little bit.

We can hold on for our blessing, hold on to our blessing, and let go of everything else. New name, new life, new way, new hope.

You can hold on in your personal life because God will see you through the times you don't think you can go through. Hold on. Having courage doesn't mean you are not scared. Real courage, the courage to hold on, means holding on in spite of the fact that we want answers and we want them now. The courage to hold on means that you can hold on even when you aren't sure how a relationship, a decision, a job, will end up. Most of us want all our ducks in a row. We want the guarantee of success. We want to be winners or we won't play the game. This is the way of the world. And the scriptures remind us, "Do not be conformed to this world, but be transformed by the renewing of your minds, so that you may discern what is the will of God—what is good and acceptable and perfect" (Romans 12:2). Hold on, just hold on and keep going, with the Lord.

In the church, hold on for your blessing. The ways of the world will tell you that a successful church is one that plays a numbers-and-dollars game. As Henry Ford once said, "Good business is good religion." Too many of us would rather follow Ford than follow the Lord. We have to remember to test ourselves and our faithfulness by the fact that we persevere for what is right, what is fair and honest and righteous. Are we trying to win a popularity contest in our own community or are we witnessing for the Kingdom and the righteousness of God?

Many churches are full because they do popular things, and they avoid any witness against the real wrongs of the world, against racism, against sexism, against all forms of oppression, simply because it's political and risks making folks grumble or leave the church. Most of the time we are more concerned about holding onto community opinion and a handful of rich and powerful families than we are about holding onto the truth of the gospel in Jesus Christ.

The faithful church will hold on for its blessings in spite of struggle, and a faithful church will not back off from a witness just because it may be painful. The Disciples congregation in my hometown of Martinsville, Indiana, is a church that is holding on, in spite of the difficulty of being a faithful witness. In a town that is notorious across the Midwest for its racism, the ministers there have started a shelter for the homeless, a thrift store, a food pantry, and a center for developing community appreciation of racial diversity. All this despite the fact that they have received criticism from inside and outside of the church. Folks are afraid the church will attract too many homeless, too many derelicts—that it will become a "mission for derelicts." They have held on to the truth and power of God when they criticized the local newspaper for its bigoted language and attitudes toward the homosexual community. The paper received a number of passionate letters blasting the church and its ministries. Threats were made against the ministers and their families, but they persisted in their witness. One of the ministers remarked, "We got very discouraged, but what we are about is the dignity and worth of all persons —created by love, created in love, created for love—so what else could we do?"

That is what we are all about. This is what Jacob's story is all about, that each and every one of us, regardless of our orneriness, our unfaithfulness, our selfishness, is a beloved and blessed child of God. This is the same truth that is witnessed in the cross of Christ, that God will keep on pouring love into the world no matter what the cost, no matter what the struggle, no matter what the setbacks. The preacher and writer Frederick Buechner says that most of us must wake up each morning to a day that we must somehow live, to a self that we must somehow be. Most of the time, he is indistinguishable from the rest of the herd that jostles and snuffles at the trough of life like a pig. But part of the time certain things seem real and important, and he recognizes Christ in other people and doesn't just see the pig in them. And then, Buechner says, a kind of heroism is momentarily possible.

So whatever you face, whatever mountains you must climb, whatever deserts you must cross, whatever valleys you must travel through, hold on. Press on. God will not leave you behind. God will not let you go, so do not let God go. Hold on, my friends; hold on, my brothers and sisters, hold on. There's a blessing in it for you. Hold on to the amazing love of God in Christ Jesus. Just reach your hand out today, get a firm grasp of the love and the power God gives, and hold on.

*I*n the middle of the wilderness

Sandra M. Messick

Sandy Morgan Messick pastors the Corydon
Christian Church, Corydon, Indiana. A graduate of
San Diego State University and Christian
Theological Seminary, she was recently ordained
in her home congregation, Vista La Mesa
Christian Church, La Mesa, California.

Exodus 16:2–15

We took our vacation at Thanksgiving that year. That in itself was unusual. Most families take their vacations in the summer and my family was no exception. But that year we decided to take a trip at Thanksgiving, a camping trip to some property my parents owned in northern California. I must have been about ten at the time and it seemed like a wonderful idea...at first.

We packed the car late Wednesday evening. We loaded the tent, the sleeping bags, the camp stove, the screen house, the portable picnic table, the food, the clothes, three dogs, four kids, and, of course, my parents, and off we went. My parents took turns during the twelve-hour drive from San Diego to the mountains north of Sacramento, arriving at our property early Thanksgiving Day. The air was fresh and crisp with a little nip in the air. It was great!

Quickly we unloaded the car, set up the tent, built the fire ring, unpacked the food...and then it was time to play. Only we four kids didn't play. We complained instead. "It's too cold," we said as we huddled in our jackets. The river was freezing; we couldn't swim there as we always did on our summer vacations. The blackberries weren't even in season. And would you be-

17

lieve: There was ice in our tire swing! Now who could enjoy a place like that? On and on we went, complaining about our misfortune, our rotten luck, our evil parents who brought us to such a place. The complaints kept coming until finally my father said, "Enough!"

He reloaded the car, repacked the tent, and the sleeping bags, and the food, three dogs, four kids, and two very tired adults. He turned the car around and drove straight home, all twelve hours, back to San Diego.

This childhood memory has some similarities to the story of the Israelites in the wilderness. A new place. A lot of complaining. Only unlike my father, God didn't turn the car around and return to Egypt. Instead, God gave the Israelites what they needed to live in that new place.

As the story begins, the Israelites find themselves wandering in the wilderness. They've escaped from Egypt and are no longer slaves! They've miraculously crossed the Red Sea (on dry land no less!) and now God is leading them through the wilderness. They're free! You'd think they'd be happy. You'd think they'd be joyous. But they weren't.

You see, all of a sudden, reality set in. The truth of their situation came and hit them in the face. Or perhaps it hit them in the belly. They were hungry. Really hungry. And suddenly these former slaves looked around and realized where they were. In the wilderness! No food, no water, no familiar landmarks. The wilderness! And in that instant, Egypt didn't look quite so bad anymore.

"If only we had died by the hand of the LORD in the land of Egypt, when we sat by the fleshpots and ate our fill of bread; for you have brought us out into this wilderness to kill this whole assembly with hunger" (Exodus 16:3). If only we had stayed in Egypt. At least there we had food and guaranteed employment—and so what if we were slaves? A little hard work never hurt anyone. And the Egyptians really weren't so bad...really.

This story hits me every time I read it, because it's just like us. It's human nature to idealize the past, especially when we find ourselves in the midst of change. The grass is always greener on the other side, and absence does make the heart grow fonder...at least in this case. In the midst of change, we cling to the familiar ways of the past.

Change is scary. It's new and it's frightening. We are creatures of habit and routine, and change can be very threatening. It really doesn't matter whether the change is good or bad, by our choice or by forces beyond ourselves; change brings stress. Whether change comes from good things such as a new home or job or the birth of a child, or whether it comes from not so good things such as the loss of a loved one or a downswing in the economy or trouble in the Middle East, no matter what the reason for the change, it brings stress. Change is scary.

And because change is scary, we tend to cling to the familiar, no matter how awful it is. Perhaps one reason why abused women and men stay in those abusive relationships is that at least they're predictable. It may not be safe or pleasant or even happy, but at least they know what to expect; at least they know the rules of the game. As the old saying goes, better the evil you know than the evil you don't. In the midst of change, when things are scary, we look to the past to give us security.

But, you see, that's the very reason that change is so scary— precisely because it does involve letting go of the past without having the present firmly in hand, like a trapeze artist who must let go of one bar before flying through the air and reaching the other bar. It's the flying through the air that gets you. That's the part that frightens us out of our wits.

Many of us know what it feels like to be flying through the air. We know, perhaps right now, that sinking feeling in our stomachs as we encounter change. As individuals, we know that fear. But as a church, we also are in the midst of change. As our churches face changing communities or declining membership or even those all too rare instances of rapid growth within a congregation, as a church we are in the midst of change. And change is just as frightening for a church as for an individual.

Now, eventually, we know that the new will become comfortable, that the Promised Land will one day be home and we will be able to let go of Egypt—at least until the next change comes along. But right now we're in the middle of change and we don't feel safe yet. In the midst of change, we're still in the wilderness, where things aren't familiar. It's as if we're driving through a snowstorm. We've left the safe haven of our homes but we haven't yet reached our destination. We're just out in the middle of nowhere, and our palms are sweaty, and our nerves are strained, and we're wishing we never ventured out here at all. The wilderness. In between Egypt and the Promised Land. And the really unfortunate thing is, you can't get from Egypt to the Promised Land without going through the wilderness. And so here we are.

And there they were. The Israelites out in the wilderness. Hungry, afraid, unsettled, looking for something they could cling to, something they could count on. And God gave it to them. God offered them food in the wilderness: quails in the evening and bread in the morning. Now granted, the bread wasn't like anything they'd seen before. When they first saw it, the Israelites questioned Moses, "What is it?" But Moses' reply told them all they needed to know. "It is the bread that the LORD has given you to eat." And from that point on, God provided that daily food—nourishment for the body and for the soul.

As Christians, we too have food in our wilderness. For us, too, God has provided an assurance of God's presence, even when everything else is strange and unfamiliar. The bread and the cup that we partake of in remembrance of Jesus is the food that nourishes our souls. It is a promise from God, as God promised the Israelites in the wilderness, that no matter what changes we go through, no matter how frightening our lives may be, God has offered us nourishment. God is present in the bread and the wine—an assurance in the midst of chaos that God has not abandoned us in the wilderness but is very real and very present, building us and supporting us and feeding us. Even now, God is leading us on to the Promised Land.

In his book *Hostage Bound, Hostage Freed*, Rev. Benjamin Wehr wrote of his experiences as a hostage in Lebanon. For part of the time, at least, Rev. Wehr was held with several other hostages. The accommodations were dismal, the future looked bleak. But as often as they could, this group worshiped God. They called their gathering "The Church of the Locked Door." Every now and again, when these hostages could salvage some bread and some liquid, they celebrated communion. And God was present. Even there, in The Church of the Locked Door, God was present. Even there, in the most dismal of wildernesses with the Promised Land only a dim hope, God was there. Even there...and even here. In the bread and in the cup, God offers to us food in the wilderness—nourishment for our journey.

*B*earing the burden

Mary Donovan Turner

Mary Donovan Turner is the newly appointed
assistant professor of homiletics at Pacific School of
Religion, the first Disciples woman to hold such a
position in an American seminary. A graduate of
Lexington Theological Seminary, she is completing
her Ph.D. in Old Testament at Candler School of
Theology, Emory University.

Numbers 11:1–25

Moses had led the people of Israel out of Egypt, and they had successfully crossed the Red Sea. The Israelites had said "yes" to the journey, and they headed out for the land of promise. They had committed themselves to travel together through the wilderness to get there. But they had no idea, I think, that the path would be such a difficult one. It was long and painful—filled with disaster and hardship.

There was little food to eat in the wilderness. The land was dry and parched, with little vegetation. Their stomachs were often gnawing with hunger. Just when they felt they could continue no longer, manna or quail would miraculously appear to sustain them. And then they could go on.

There was little water in the wilderness. When it appeared that they could not take one more step without fluids to quench their thirst, the Lord would supply a steady flow from a rock. And then they could go on.

There were hostile and warring enemy tribes in the wilderness who seemed to come out of nowhere—tribes that blocked the way to the land of milk and honey, tribes that were prepared to fight to the death. Moses would take the rod of the Lord in his hand and raise it, and miraculously,

21

against all odds, the Israelites would win. And then they could go on.

It appeared that no matter what obstacle their community would encounter, they were blessed in wondrous ways with whatever they needed to keep on "keeping on." Perhaps most importantly, they were given the gift of the powerful and capable guidance of their leader, Moses. Who really could ask for more? Moses seemed to have it all.

The story tells us how very special Moses was, even from the moment of his birth. From the very moment when he was rescued by the princess from the waters of the river, he seemed to be chosen for the task that would lie before him. And it was Moses who was so special in the eyes of the Lord that he alone was called to go up to the top of Mt. Sinai to receive the law that became so very important to the Israelite people. No one was allowed to go up the mountain or even touch the border of it. "Anyone who touches the mountain will be put to death," said the Lord. Anyone but the great Moses. Moses was so blessed by God, the scriptures tell us, that he lived to the age of one hundred twenty. He was buried in the land of Moab at a place no one knew. The book of Deuteronomy tells us that there was no other prophet in Israel like Moses, whom the Lord knew "face to face."

When we read about this dangerous and tedious journey of the Israelite people and about the leader chosen to guide them through the wilderness, we think, "If our congregation had a leader like Moses, if our church had a leader chosen from infancy to be a servant, if we just had a leader so close to the Lord that the Lord knew her 'face to face,' if we had this one-of-a-kind leader like no other—then our community would make it to the Promised Land too."

"So where are they?" I hear people in the churches asking. "Where are these great women and men of faith like the ones we read about in our Old and New Testaments. Where are those decisive, competent individuals who led the people of God to prosperity and growth?"

Longingly we look back and remember the faithful Abraham who seemed to have *no* limit to what he was willing to do for the Lord, the Abraham who heeded the call to sacrifice his own son for whom he had waited for almost a hundred years...and Deborah, who courageously led her people down Mt. Tabor to victory...the loving Ruth, who, in her own assertive way, would show the world what love and loyalty were all about...the forceful Paul, who, after his conversion, could not work long enough or hard enough in taking the "good news" from city to city...the women of the early church. And on and on the list goes, of dedicated, loyal, faithful, and courageous leaders who were called to lead the people of God.

"Where are they?" the churches are asking. They are searching fervently for those *single, solitary* individuals who can lead their communities in celebrating the past that has been and the future that will be. The churches are looking for those who can speak the prophetic word of the Lord and lead their congregations through the wilderness. "We want our leader!" the congregations are saying. "We want our Moses."

But there are some things that we have forgotten. We forget that even though the story tells us that Moses was chosen from birth and received an incredible call at the site of the burning bush, he did not want the job. "I'm not capable," he said. "The people will not believe me. I am slow of speech. Please, please, please send another."

And we forget that although Moses seemed to be empowered with all the authority we would ever want—he had possession of that powerful rod that would work miracles, knew his Lord face to face, provided wisdom to settle disputes (and 600,000 people traveling together are bound to have a few disputes!)—even so, the community was not always satisfied with his leadership. Immediately after the people followed Moses out of Egypt where they had been shrewdly and horribly oppressed, they complained bitterly about the life with which Moses had presented them. No cucumbers, no leeks, no garlic. No water. They had expected this new leader to provide them with instant passage to the new world. They expected to replace the life they had led before with a life of ease and immediate prosperity. But that was not to be. Their journey together was one of searching and discovery, with slow and painful steps to their destination. Not even a Moses could automatically deliver them to the land of their dreams.

And we forget that, for Moses, sometimes the task of leading God's people was just too great. Moses was in the wilderness. The people were encamped there. He heard the families of his congregation standing at the door of their tents. They were mourning and weeping. The journey was too hard.

"We have this manna to eat," they said, "but we long for the meat we had in Egypt. With nothing but his manna to eat, our strength is all gone. We wish we had never made this journey after all." Moses heard this complaining at the tent doors, and he was angry—not at the people, but at the Lord.

"Why did you do this to me?" he asked. "Why did you put all this burden on me? It is too much. These aren't my children! These are your children! I didn't conceive them. Do you think I should nurse them along till we get where we're going? I can't do it!" Moses said. "This burden is too great. Do me a favor. Do away with my life, because I am not capable of leading your people. I can't stand my misery."

And the Lord looked down and said, "I know, Moses. I know that you can't lead the people of God alone. So I'll tell you what to do. Gather for me some of your people and take them to your place of worship. I'll come down and talk with you there. I'll take a little of that special spirit that I poured upon your life, and I'll pour it upon them. They will help you bear the burden of the journey. And I'll be with you. I'll give your people meat to eat. Not enough for one day or two or five or ten or twenty, but more. You'll have so much to eat that food will become disgusting to you."

"Food for a month?" asked Moses. "There are 600,000 people out there, and you say you'll feed us? It would take all the flocks and herds and all the fish in the sea to satisfy my congregation!"

"Moses, Moses, Moses," the Lord said. "Don't you remember how I watched over you when you were small? Don't you remember how I watched over you and protected you on your journey? How I gave you food and water, and led you to victory over those enemy tribes? Do you think now my hand is shortened? Do you think I can't reach down and nestle you in the palm of my hand?"

Well, Moses went out and gathered the people and put them around the place of worship, and that morning the spirit of the Lord came down and rested on them all. They began to pray and prophesy. They began to celebrate and share the presence of the Lord in ways they never had before. And then the people couldn't complain about the journey because the burden and the responsibility of the trip were upon them. And Moses needed not feel burdened by the responsibility because other hands had been blessed to help him.

It was then, and only then, with the burden for the journey not on the shoulders of one but shared by all, that the Israelites could pick up stakes and begin again the journey that eventually led them to the land of promise.

One *single, solitary* individual to lead your congregation, to lead the church on its journey of faith? No. The burden is everyone's to share.

*F*or such a time as this

Nancy Claire Pittman

Nancy Claire Pittman is a doctoral candidate in
New Testament at Southern Methodist University.
Her undergraduate and M.Div. degrees
are from Texas Christian University. This sermon
was preached on a hot July Sunday morning at
Oak Cliff Christian Church of Dallas, Texas, where
Nancy was serving as associate minister, and is
dedicated to the people of that congregation.

Esther 4:13–17

Esther must have been beautiful—young and beautiful, for she had won the Persian equivalent of the Miss Universe pageant. Instead of winning a scholarship, hundreds of prizes, and a modeling contract, Esther was made queen to the king of the known universe. This king is called Ahasuerus in the scripture, but he is often identified with the historical figure Xerxes, emperor of the Medes and the Persians. Several years before our story opens, he had conquered the Babylonians—who, in their time of world power, had conquered Israel and brought a number of Jews into exile. That is how the Jewess Esther and her cousin Mordecai had come to be in the Persian Empire.

At first glance, it would seem that Esther had won herself a great job. All she had to do was keep herself beautiful just in case the king came to visit her or summoned her to his side. She also had to remember that her predecessor, Vashti, was dethroned for disobediently refusing to come to the king upon his command. Kings' courts being what they were in those days, however, it soon became apparent that Esther's job was not going to be a spring picnic.

You see, Ahasuerus had a wicked prime minister, Haman the Agagite, who hated the Jews and was searching for a way

25

to exterminate them. Although he didn't know that Esther was Jewish, he knew that Mordecai was, and it infuriated him that Mordecai would not bow down, like everyone else, when he passed by. Finally, his vanity bruised to its limits, Haman hatched a plot in which he told the king that there was an evil people in the realm doing everything they could to bring about his overthrow. Ahasuerus, of course, was alarmed at this news. In a smooth and oily way, Haman assured the king that, with his permission, he and his relatives, the Agagites, could get rid of this rebellious people. Since the king continued to nod along, Haman flourished a paper in front of him, said "Sign here and stamp there!" and went off to rejoice wickedly in the knowledge that once the king signed and sealed a decree, it could not be revoked. The king had just signed a decree that stated that the Jews were to be defenselessly destroyed on a certain day in eleven months. The plot thickens.

Once Mordecai got wind of the decree, he donned sackcloth and ashes, the traditional costume of sorrow and mourning for the Jews, hurried to Esther's palace, and demanded to see her, telling the servants to give her the news about the evil decree. Upon hearing the story and a description of Mordecai's dress, Esther sent him fresh clothes and word that she could do nothing.

A word in Esther's defense is in order at this point. Her reluctance to get involved may have been based on emotions we know quite well. Obviously, she was afraid. Even if there weren't a threat of physical violence against her, by taking any action on behalf of her people, she ran the risk of losing the acceptance that was hers with the king and the king's court. How many times have we avoided doing the right thing out of fear of rejection? How many times have we been content to accept the status quo for fear of losing esteem or favor in someone's eyes?

Moreover, she may have had a sense of personal worthlessness that hindered her from positive action. What can I, a mere woman, do that would possibly improve the situation? How many times have we said to ourselves, and sincerely believed it, that we were too insignificant or had too few skills or abilities to right wrongs, to seek justice for others, to show compassion to another? If we answer that at least once we have felt these things, then we must have some sympathy for Esther and her predicament.

Mordecai, however, had no patience whatsoever with her. Again through messengers, Mordecai reminded Esther that she was also Jewish and therefore not exempt from the death Haman had planned. Moreover, even if she refused to help, something or someone would save the Jews—but because of her sinful refusal, she would not be included in that salvation. And then Mordecai asked, "Who knows? Perhaps you have come to royal dignity for just such a time as this" (Esther 4:14b).

Esther was convinced. She sent word to Mordecai to tell all the Jews to fast with her for three days, and then she put on her own sackcloth and ashes and began to design a plan to save her people. In order to get the king's attention, she would go before him, unsummoned.

Remember, one queen had already been deposed for disobedience. So it took some courage for Esther to go before the king uninvited. But after two days of fasting, she exchanged her sackcloth for her finest dress and proceeded to his audience hall. If, when she appeared, he held out his scepter to her, she would be received. But if he did not hold out the scepter, she would be killed immediately. Novels have been written about this pregnant moment. Will he or won't he? Like any good romance, the king receives his beloved and the scene for the last act is set.

At the audience, she invited Ahasuerus and Haman to dinner that night. Over dinner she invited them to return the next evening. Haman was beside himself with pride and joy. Ahasuerus promised anything, as much as half of his kingdom, to his queen. So at dinner on the second night, she revealed Haman's lie about the insidiousness of the Jews and the fact that she herself was Jewish. The king was enraged over Haman's trickery and ordered him executed. Then, because a Persian king's decree could not be revoked, even by the king himself, he wrote a new decree giving the Jews the right to defend themselves on the appointed day.

And so, eleven months later, the Jews fought their ancient enemies, the Agagites, and won the day. Esther and her cousin Mordecai saved their people.

For a number of reasons this book was almost left out of the Bible by both Jewish and Christian compilers. It has, in fact, caused considerable controversy over the years. The book has been repeatedly described as bloodthirsty and nationalistic, presenting a picture of a people determined to find any way they could to save themselves, with or without God. But the book was finally left in place because there are lessons to be learned in the story of Esther.

First, Esther, in spite of her great beauty, was no one special in and of herself. Her first response to Mordecai's news was a refusal to get involved in this sordid business. Moreover, she tried to ignore the problem, even to the point of sending Mordecai fresh clothes as though his sackcloth and ashes were something he put on because he didn't have anything else to wear. As I implied earlier, we know what it feels like to be reluctant to get involved, afraid to upset the delicate equilibrium of our lives to take up some job that needs doing, to help friends or strangers, to face up to what is evil around us instead of trying so hard to lock it out of our lives. We have also believed that our own obscurity or insignificance wasn't good enough for God, forgetting that God is good enough to compensate for any ability or talent we might lack.

Second, either through fear of the consequences or an overpowering sense of faith, Esther came to realize that she was answerable to a greater reality than the king of Persia. Now, you may already know that the name of God is not mentioned one time in the entire book. That fact has been the strongest argument for excluding it from the canon. But J.G. McConville explains the absence of the name of God in this way:

> There are many coincidences in the book that appear to be historical causes and effects, nothing more. Vashti is disobedient, Esther is made queen in her place. The decree goes out against the Jews because Mordecai refuses to bow down to Haman. But all these coincidences point to a deeper reality—the providence of God. The silence about God in the book is quite deliberate, not to make the point that God is inactive in human situations, but, on the contrary, that God is hidden behind all events.[1]

Somehow, in the midst of the crisis, Esther remembered God's providence and forgot herself for the sake of her people. We too know that God is ruler of all of life, and that God, though often hidden, works in all the world—sustaining, creating, redeeming. The question then for us is not just whether we affirm that truth, but how we allow it to work in our lives. Will we be a part of God's plans? Will we open ourselves to any possibility in service to the Lord of life, no matter how great or how small, or will we choose instead to sit outside of God's purposes? We face these questions every day in a multitude of circumstances.

Third, when Esther finally decided that she would rise to the occasion, she took some time to gather the necessary resources around her. Fasting is a sign of devotion and prayer, so although prayer is not specifically mentioned in the book, we can assume that she, and all the Jews with her, turned first to God in this hour of tribulation. They turned to the One who had always been there for them, from the pilgrimage of Abraham and Sarah to the long, hot trek across the desert when Israel was destroyed by the Babylonians.

Spiritual preparation is necessary when we make ourselves a part of God's purposes. Strength and courage do not merely come to us until we take the time to find them outside ourselves in God. Sometimes we prepare most of our lives, because we do not know when we will be called upon to be strong and courageous.

So in the fourth lesson in the story of Esther, Esther did not know that God placed her in the king's palace to save the Jews. She didn't know what action of hers might be a part of God's plan. And neither do we always know. Not only do we not know when we will be needed, but we do not always know what action of ours will be the right thing to do at the right time. Who knows when our patience or energy or persistence will inspire another? Who knows when some small kindness of our own will blossom into mercy or justice for others? Who knows what the acceptance of God's call in your life will change in the lives of others, some of whom you may never know? Who can measure what God can and will accomplish through the lives of ordinary people?

In 1957 Central High School in Little Rock, Arkansas, was the focus of national attention and turmoil as a previously all-white school prepared to integrate black youth into its student body. I have felt somehow connected to that historical moment ever since I discovered that my good friend Bert Cartwright, the retired area minister of the Trinity Brazos Area of the Christian Church in the Southwest, was significantly involved in the events of that summer and fall. Those of you who are old enough or have seen various accounts of the story of those days may remember the pictures of the first day of school when the nine black kids who lived in the district tried to enter. One young, black fourteen-year-old girl got separated from the others and the angry mob closed in upon her. She was yelled at, cursed, spit upon, and shoved about. But she finally got home. That night, as a local minister in suburban Little Rock, Bert made a pastoral visit upon her and her family. And he asked her how in the world she got through those moments. "Faith in Jesus," she replied. And the next day, and all the days following, she went back to Central High to get an education. The following Sunday, Bert preached a sermon entitled "Portrait of Courage in Ebony." Some members left the church over that sermon, but most stayed. Bert became one of the few white people in Little Rock with whom the black civil rights leaders would work in 1957. He was a mediator, a representative of God's mercy and love for all people in an incendiary situation. And the fourteen-year-old girl? I don't know what became of her personally. I can't even remember her name. But we all know the good things that her courage and the courage of hundreds and thousands of people across this nation accomplished in those very troubled times.

Faith in Jesus. Faith in the One who sent Jesus, who sent all those who came before Jesus: Esther, Sarah and Abraham, Ruth, David, Jeremiah. Faith in the One who sent all who came with and after Jesus: Mary, Peter, Paul, Phoebe. Faith in the One who sends us. For the work is not over. There is plenty for everyone to do in the effort to proclaim the death and resurrection of our Lord to the world, to declare his victory over evil and death and his sovereignty in the world. Let us then remember what has been done before us, and let us prepare ourselves to participate in the service of God—both in the little circumstances of our daily living and in those unknown moments when God is counting on us to do the right thing. For who knows whether you, or I, have been born for such a time as this. Amen.

---

[1]J.G. McConville, *Ezra, Nehemiah, and Esther.* Westminster Press, 1985, p. 153.

$\mathcal{P}$rophetic patience

Stephanie Paulsell

Stephanie Paulsell is an ordained Disciples of
Christ minister and a doctoral student in religion
and literature at the University of Chicago Divinity
School. This sermon was preached during her
tenure as chaplain at the University of Chicago's
Rockefeller Chapel. The sermon is dedicated to
Sister Cornelia Berry, OJN, whose
friendship inspired it.

Isaiah 35:1–10; James 5:7–10; Matthew 11:2–11

"Be patient, therefore, beloved, until the coming of the Lord"
(James 5:7a).

The traditional Advent theme of patience is a very attractive one for me, but one that I find remarkably difficult to integrate into these four weeks. If I am very busy, Christmas sneaks up on me before I've made adequate preparations, and Advent rushes past with feelings of haste, not patience. If—and this happens very rarely—I have prepared gifts and cards and food well in advance, I find myself waiting somewhat impatiently: for the excitement of traveling, for time off from school and work, for the gathering of family and friends. Often I find myself saying after Christmas, "Next year I will slow down during Advent. Next year I will reflect on what being 'patient until the coming of the Lord' might mean."

But the theme of patience does not carry with it merely the attractive connotations of quiet reflection and intentional preparation. Patience has a darker side that also bears examining during Advent. Biblical passages such as the exhortation in the Letter of James to be patient until the Lord comes have often been used to encourage complacency and passivity. Liberation theologies have exposed the evil of admonishing the poor and

31

oppressed to "be patient" when that means "accept your lot without complaint, because you'll be better off in the next world." The notion of patience has often been used as a weapon by those who wish to preserve unequal systems of privilege. American slaves were told to be patient. Women have been told to be patient: One day you'll be able to vote, one day perhaps you'll be able to be ordained, but only when the rest of the world is ready. Just be patient. Black South Africans and those in solidarity with them are told that apartheid will surely end, but only when the time is right. Just be patient. Thank God that so many of our sisters and brothers have resisted this sort of "patience"!

But does this mean that patience is not a valid theological concept for us? By no means. To equate patience with acquiescence is a terrible misuse of the word, as the author of the Letter of James implies. Two images of patience are offered to us in the reading from the Letter of James, images that suggest its deeply prophetic meaning. The first is the image of the farmer. "The farmer," our author writes, "waits for the precious crop from the earth, being patient with it until it receives the early and the late rains" (James 5:7b). The second image is that of the prophet. As an example of patience, we read, "take the prophets who spoke in the name of the Lord" (James 5:10).

Those of us who have been meeting in the chancel for the daily service of Morning Prayer have been reading for the past two weeks of Advent from the book of the prophet Amos. Amos tells us that he was called by God from his work as a shepherd to preach an angry message to the most difficult audience a prophet can have: a thriving, prosperous people. The voice of God roars in Amos, cataloging the sins of God's people and promising swift and severe punishment. It has not been comfortable these past few weeks to listen to Amos speak of God's anger and disappointment. Patience is definitely not a word I would have chosen to describe Amos and his message. Nor does it seem to apply to the ministry of John the Baptist, who preached repentance with an impatient urgency, and who, in today's reading from the Gospel of Matthew, sends messengers to Jesus to ask if he is the one whom John has announced or whether John and his followers should look for another. John's insistent need to be sure of Jesus' authority hardly seems a model for patience.

So what can the author of the Letter of James mean when he commends to us the patience of the prophets? They seem to be the most impatient characters of all. And in many ways they are, for they are impatient with injustice and hypocrisy and with wasting time. God is impatient with your burnt offerings and sacrifices, says Amos, and wants justice to roll down like waters—now! When John the Baptist impatiently sends his followers to Jesus, he seems to say, I have work to do in proclaiming the Kingdom, so if you are not the one, I must know and waste no time looking for the true Messiah.

John does not say, however, that if Jesus is not the promised Messiah he will give up, that he will stop his condemnation of Herod and Herodias and Philip and thereby save his own life. And that is what I think the author of the Letter of James must have meant when he tells us to look to the prophets if we want to understand what true patience is. It is the patience of Amos who refused to flee or be quiet, even when threatened by the king's own priest, but who remains steadfast, preaching difficult words in an easy time. It is the patience of John the Baptist, who kept his eyes firmly fixed on the coming of God, even when troubled by his own doubts. It is the patience of the prophet Anna, who remained in the temple for years upon years, worshiping God with prayer and fasting in order to be ready when the child of God appeared.

It is the kind of patience we still see around us in our own world—not a patience that accepts situations passively, but the patience of Father Ignacio Martin-Baro and his colleagues in El Salvador, impatient with the injustice they saw around them, but endlessly patient in their steadfastness to their vocation of combatting that injustice, even in the face of death. It is what Simone Weil meant when she talked about "waiting in patience" for God—that is, positioning oneself in God's direction, keeping one's head turned toward God, just as sin involves turning one's gaze away from God. "Strengthen your hearts, for the coming of the Lord is near," writes the author of the Letter of James (5:8). The patience of the prophets that the writer extols is precisely a prophetic patience—a patience that arises from a heart established in God, a lived patience that gives witness to God's mercy and to the expectation of a time when God's justice will be lived to the full.

But the prophets are not the only examples of patience offered by the author of the Letter of James. We are also invited to observe the farmer. "The farmer waits for the precious crop from the earth, being patient with it until it receives the early and the late rains" (James 5:7b). The coming of God for which we wait—no less precious or nourishing than the farmer's ripening crop—is portrayed here not as some sort of dramatic entrance, but as something organic, something growing up all around us. Growing like the fruit of the earth. Growing like a baby in a woman's womb. Waiting for fruit to ripen, or for a baby to be born, requires a different sort of patience than waiting for a sudden surprise out of nowhere. Both require a prophetic patience, surely. But the patience of Advent is also the patience of the farmer. It is a patience that works at cultivation, a patience that tends.

Farmers, of course, have fields and gardens and trees that they tend. The field we are called upon to care for during Advent is the fruitful field of the prophets: the desert. The desert seems an unlikely place in which to nurture growth, but it has been a fertile garden for many of our ancestors. The monks who followed St. Antony into the desert understood the desert's fertility. The desert was the place where they went to battle their demons and make their souls. In the *Life of St. Antony,* written by his admirer Anthansius of Alexandria, even Satan is reported to have complained, "I no longer have a place to roam freely—even the desert is full of monks!"

The life of the desert is sometimes thought of as a giving up, a withdrawal from the world. If anything, however, the desert-dwellers have plunged more deeply into life than many who have remained "in the world." They expose themselves to the world and to themselves and to God directly, not cushioned all around by what Virginia Woolf calls the "cotton wool of non-being" that keeps us from the presence of the real. And in facing the world in the barrenness of the desert, they draw the world to them.

John the Baptist certainly understood this. It was to the desert that John went to "prepare a way for the Lord," and by living on the boundary, he challenged the center, a challenge that would change the lives of many and cost him his own. "What did you go out into the wilderness to look at?" Jesus asked the crowds who sought him out because John had told them to. "A reed shaken by the wind? What then did you go out to see? Someone dressed in soft robes? Look, those who wear soft robes are in royal palaces. What then did you go out to see? A prophet? Yes, I tell you, and more than a prophet. This is the one about whom it is written,

'See, I am sending my messenger ahead of you, who will prepare your way before you'" (Matthew 11:7-10).

Prophets tend the desert with the patience of farmers who nurture the soil and what the soil bears within it.

Although we are all called to a prophetic patience, we are not all called to the desert as Antony or John understood it. What, then, is the desert we must tend this Advent? The beautiful prophecy from Isaiah, which we heard this morning, may give us some help. Isaiah 35 offers us a vision of the earth, healed and reborn. The desert blossoms, streams break forth in the wilderness, burning sands become cool pools of water. The desert that has separated God's people from their homeland does not disappear in this vision. Instead, it becomes fertile and rich.

This is the field that we must tend as vigilant farmers—the vast, dry spaces that separate us from God, both those deserts in our own souls and those that mar the world around us. Such cultivation will require courage, for it will take us into places where God seems utterly absent. And it will require patience, both the bold patience of the prophets and the steadfast patience of the farmer and the woman who bears a child within her body. Both must offer their own protective care, but both must also trust the mysterious process of growth over which they seem to have no control.

When we water the loveless places in our lives and in our world, we must not expect them to disappear, but to become transformed into places where we meet God. They will become an open, unimpeded road to God, over which even the most wounded of exiles can travel safely.

Amen.

Strange messengers

Karen Leigh Stroup

Karen Leigh Stroup currently resides in the
Capitol area where she is engaged in a variety of
ministries. She graduated from the University of
North Carolina with highest honors in religious
studies, where she was inducted into
Phi Beta Kappa, and went on to earn the M.Div.
from Lexington Theological Seminary. Karen has
served Disciples congregations in Winchester
and Pleasureville, Kentucky.

Luke 2:8–20

Christmas morning was strange for me this year. Actually,
the whole season was different than usual, starting with Advent. Being in seminary puts a whole new slant on things. Just
about the first week of Advent, when most people were buying
gifts and trimming trees, my fellow students and I were studying for finals, searching for the last few references for the
research paper, and thinking an awful lot about going home.
The seminary closes down over Christmas, so there were very
few decorations up to give us an idea of what was coming. Then
the last day of exams was over and the place emptied out. I think
there were two people in my entire dormitory the last week I
was there. Of course, I spent a good amount of time at work at
First Christian Church in Winchester, and certainly we had
decorations and Christmas projects, but that made it seem, in
a funny way, that people were preparing for Christmas over in
Winchester, but that Lexington was in a time warp where
Christmas was not going to arrive.

I was going to be working on Christmas morning, but
worship did not start until 10:45. I do not care how old I get, I
still wake up early on Christmas, and what in the world was I
going to do with those hours, waiting to go to church and then

take off for home? I did not want to be sitting around thinking of all the happy families waking up together to celebrate Christmas. I needed something to do before church!

I tell you this because I do not want you to think that it was any noble motivation that drove me to the Community Kitchen at 5 a.m. on Christmas morning. I have a friend who is the cook there, and he suspected that the church groups that usually staff the place would not be interested in coming out on Christmas morning, so they would need some help preparing the meal. This was *just* the opportunity: The Kitchen needed someone to cook and serve, and I needed some way to pass the time until worship.

It was still dark when I got there, of course, and the doors were already open and the hall was packed with men and women waiting for the meal that would not be served until 9 o'clock. I have never seen so much cigarette smoke in my life. It hung like a fog over the whole room, despite an industrial-sized fan that recirculated the air. And there was, in the room, the sour, unmistakable smell of the morning after a heavy drunk. Some people were just sleeping in the warmth, but others were playing cards or hanging around, talking. As I worked my way through the group, in my Christmas church clothes, I was greeted with lots of "Hey, mamas" and kissing sounds and invitations that I will not repeat here.

I was very glad to get back to the kitchen, which was locked against the people outside, and to see the familiar face of my friend. I put on an apron and started making soup, mashed potatoes, and chicken livers by the gallon. I would take a big handful of chicken livers and lift them out of the bowl, then squeeze them to let the extra blood run off, then throw them into some cornmeal and finally onto a baking sheet. A couple of times I thought to myself, "Is this Christmas?" but I put that out of my mind quickly and concentrated on the cooking. About 8:30 I started setting up the serving line, and by that time the room was packed. We would serve 250 meals that morning, in a city with fewer than 200,000 people.

You know, I think it is very important that we begin paying attention to the problems of homelessness in our country. It is a big problem and a serious one. But you see, we do not need to romanticize these victims of society either. Let me tell you, there is nothing romantic about them. There are a lot of them, and they smell and they are dirty and they are drunk and some of them are simply, purely, undeniably crazy. Outside the safety of the locked kitchen, I felt exposed, a little threatened by the ones who kept coming up and demanding food, a little overwhelmed by the smell. I did the best I could and raised up a tiny little prayer: "Dear God, how do I find Christmas in all of this?"

I wonder the same thing about Mary. Jesus' mother gets just a small mention in the Gospel reading today. "But Mary treasured all these words and pondered them in her heart," it says (Luke 2:19). Now, *pondered* is not exactly a word filled with connotations of joy. It gives more of the sense of "What is going on here?" And I imagine that Mary had more than a little bit of confusion to deal with that Christmas morning.

The first part of today's Gospel lesson tells us about the shepherds coming to the stable, seeing the Christ child, and telling his parents about the message they had received from the angels. Many of us have a crèche at home, and there are usually shepherds in it. If we look closely at the shepherd figures, we find that they are young; chances are they're fairly handsome, dressed in some sort of caveman fur draped over one shoulder, maybe carrying lambs around their necks, reminding us of the story Jesus would later tell about the good shepherd. We imagine the shepherds brushing the grass out of their hair, trooping off to Bethlehem, bringing into the stable a breath of fresh air from the open fields, and adoring the Christ child with a simple but profound understanding of what is going on. Ah, sweet, dear shepherds.

But this is where Mary's puzzlement comes in. Because Mary was a good Jewish girl of her time, and she knew very well the kind of reputation that shepherds had. It was *not* sweet and dear. Shepherds were seen as the lowest of the low, maybe something akin to how we see child molesters today. They were despised, considered to be thieves, dishonest, violent, dangerous men. They were not allowed to testify in court—everyone knew shepherds lied all the time. Shepherds were not the salt of the earth but rather the scum of the earth, and suddenly here is poor Mary surrounded by them.

Young Mary, maybe fifteen years old by this time, who has almost lost a husband by becoming pregnant by God, who has had to put up with the gossip and scorn of her friends and townspeople for the sin of adultery—because, after all, though Joseph received a dream explaining all of this, we cannot assume that everyone who ever knew Mary received the same dream. Then a long, hard pregnancy, ending in an arduous trip to Bethlehem, bedding down with the animals in a stable, exhausted, wanting nothing but a good night's sleep. And the labor pains come, awakening her, and she goes through all the fear of a first birth without the comfort of her mother or a midwife.

Finally the baby is born, and she collapses back, exhausted, holding him close to her and feeling that the presence of this small being really does make up for a lot. The worst is over; he has been born, and sooner or later they will all go home. The folks in town will get used to the idea, and life will return to normal. And maybe Mary's mind wanders back to the beginning of all this, to the Annunciation, when that presence came upon her and she was told that she would bear the Son of David, those long-understood Jewish words for the Messiah. She would live to see this tiny child grow up to become the King, to reign in a splendid palace, to throw off the oppression under which the Jews had suffered for so long. This is what everyone knew about the Messiah, right? And this might be an inauspicious beginning, but...well, all that would make up for this. By the time her son stepped up to the throne, with crowds singing his praises, all this peculiarity surrounding his birth would be a dim memory. Yes, the worst was over.

And then, suddenly, Mary is back to reality and even this mean and dirty stable is not theirs alone any more. A group of men enter, talking excitedly, and Mary can tell from their dress and from their smell that they are shepherds. Her mother has always warned her about these types, and she has always given them a wide berth in the streets of Nazareth when they come into town for supplies. Yet here they are, so many of them, and she is exhausted. Are they going to try to hurt her and her baby? She calms her heart enough so that the pounding in her head quiets and she listens to what they are saying. Angels? The Christ is born? A singing multitude? Oh, please, these are shepherds, and they have probably been drinking to keep themselves warm, imagining all sorts of things.

And yet...and yet: Mary has had firsthand experience with an angel. These men seem to know what they are talking about. And they are here, right? How did they know to come here, how did they know how to find them, and why is the message they have been told so amazingly close to the one that she herself heard? Is it possible? But why would God choose these, these...*scum* to bring this message? Somehow this "inauspicious" beginning is staying strange, unlike what you would expect for a child who would one day reign over the world. What is going on here? Is this Christmas?

I suspect sometimes that our God has a bizarre sense of humor. I mean, here is Mary—poor, tired Mary—expecting, if any visitors, some more like the three kings who will happen by later. Now *that* makes sense, given who the Messiah is to be. But she is not going to be able to forget these shepherds, either, and the question is going to be how to put the two together, how to figure it all out. What does this mean for her son, this Jesus, the Christ? What is going on here?

God sends us strange messengers too. I cannot tell you how many times I have prayed for a burning bush—or at least a burning twig—or if not for the actual presence of God, at least Gabriel. Some shining messenger with a straightforward message from the Most High. I often find that I am looking so hard for these...well, these Godly signs that I miss the ones God sends.

Well, back to the Community Kitchen. We finally started serving the meal, and thanks be to God a group from the local synagogue showed up to help. I made about three gallons of salad dressing in the kitchen and scurried out front to put it on the condiments table. An old man was waiting there, expired fast-food salad in hand, watching me set down the huge bowl and stick the spoon in it. He was, I saw, actually not so old, but his beard was gray and the wrinkles in his face were deep. And I want to tell you, he smelled. I could smell him from six feet away. His clothes were not just stained, but they were dirty from thread to thread, dirt ground in and turning everything a mud brown. He had a thread of drool that came out of one side of his mouth, and his beard was stained orange from its track.

Suddenly he put down his salad and grabbed me by the arm. He was small, but very strong. I pulled against him for a second, and then got control over myself. "What is it?" I asked, and made myself look into his eyes.

He had only one or two teeth and a thick eastern Kentucky accent, so he was hard to understand. "It's Christmas, ain't it?" He asked. "Ain't it?"

It was a fair question. I knew these folks probably lost track of time, and the rabbi with the volunteers had said grace, so there had certainly been no mention of Jesus. "Yes," I said. "Merry Christmas."

He dropped my arm, put both his hands on his stomach, and threw back his head and laughed. "I knew it," he said. "I jist knew it. God came to me last night and he told me. I've got the baby Jesus growing in me right here. Right here. I can feel him kick."

What could I say? I went back to the kitchen to make some more chicken livers. Crazy old man. Nuts. Completely gone. Right? I mean, who has ever had a messenger like that?

Merry Christmas.

$\mathcal{S}$oil and water

Charlotte Nabors

> *Charlotte Nabors* is associate minister at
> Central Christian Church in Dallas, Texas. A
> graduate of Furman University and the University
> of St. Thomas, she holds the D.Min. degree from
> Brite Divinity School. Charlotte has served the
> church's global mission by teaching Christian
> education at the Thailand Theological Seminary
> and conducting workshops and seminars
> throughout southeast Asia.

Romans 6:1–4 and Acts 2:22–24, 32, 36–39

Baptism. That is our focus for the Lenten season that begins today, on Ash Wednesday. We are seeking to renew the baptismal covenants most of us made long ago. This theme underlies the work that I do with Central Christian Church's young adults. We spent an exciting weekend last Friday and Saturday in a retreat setting. We sat around a crackling fire in a lodge and told stories—stories of our baptisms. It was interesting—some immersed right here in this church, some elsewhere, some sprinkled. For most of us, to tell the story of our baptism was the beginning step to discovering what that so-little-understood sacrament now means for our lives.

One youth told of being sprinkled along with his twin brother. He wore a little white silk suit in which an older brother had also been baptized, and he had a little white pair of shoes and was wrapped in an all-white blanket made especially for him and for the occasion. He hadn't thought much about it until he called his mom to ask the details of his baptism. White, all white, white of purity and cleanliness—that's how he had been brought to the baptismal font.

That's how we come into the baptistry, too. Not in regular street clothes, but white robed.

I remember when I was baptized. I was almost twelve. It was April, the new-life time of the year; back where I'm from, spring comes slowly. I didn't get baptized with others of my age, with Margaret, Sara Ann, or Freddie. In fact, I don't remember their baptism. I only remember that my mother wouldn't let me. Baptism was a serious matter to take place between me and the Jesus I would claim and was not to be one more child dunked in the water. I needed to know what it meant.

I thought that I knew what it meant and that what I believed about Jesus was real. I'd been brought up in the church; I had a Christian family. I was old enough to make up my own mind. I was sorry for my sins. What more did I need?

But whenever, however, my friends were baptized, I was not among them.

It was while that was still fresh on my mind that we—Margaret, Sara Ann, Freddie; I don't remember who else; probably Nancy and Jimmy, they were older—went to a youth rally one Sunday evening in a city an hour or so from home. My father drove us.

I don't remember what we did except fellowship with kids from other churches, and probably eat, and surely some other things too. I only remember the closing worship service—at least one part of it. Someone brought the message and offered an invitation to make the confession of faith. I don't remember who it was, but he must have sounded like the voice of Jesus because before I even realized what was happening to me, I was sliding past my dad on the pew beside me and going forward.

I could not keep myself from going, although somewhere in the back of my head were my mother's words that I might not be ready yet and somewhere in my heart some guilt that I had not saved that very sacred moment to be shared with all my family and my church family.

"Do you believe that Jesus is the Christ, the Son of the living God, and do you accept him as your Lord and Savior?" I heard the voice ask me. "I do," I heard my own quivering voice reply.

On the way home, I was both excited by the experience and afraid of facing Mother. What would she say? My father and I were close, as girls and their daddies can often be. He would understand. Besides, he was there when it happened and we talked about it in the car on the way home. I trusted he'd make it all right. He did. Or something did. Mother raised no voice of protest. I guess she understood, too.

Dr. Donaldson, my minister, came to see me one afternoon very soon after that. We had our own private pastor's class in my room. I remember that he asked me my six favorite hymns. One of them was "Living for Jesus a Life That Is True." A second was "I Would Be True" and another "Are Ye Able?" I remember that he prayed with me and for me and I felt very warm and special.

It must have been only a Sunday or two later that I put on a white robe and stepped down into the baptismal waters framed by deep wine-velvet curtains. Dr. Donaldson reached out his steady hand to take hold of my trembling one and to guide me to him. A handkerchief was in my other hand. I held it up to keep it dry. After all, there was no need to have a wet handkerchief to protect my nose from the water.

"Do you believe that Jesus is the Christ, the Son of the living God, and do you take him as your Lord and Savior?" My church family got to hear my confession this time, although I suspect my "I do" was too soft to travel much farther than the third row where my father and younger brother and sister—and, of course, my mother—were sitting.

With one motion, Dr. Donaldson placed one hand under my two, trying to keep my handkerchief dry, and raised the other high into the air. He looked up and announced, as if he were telling Jesus himself, "I now baptize you in the name of the Father, the Son, and the Holy Spirit. Amen." In the next quick movement his hand clasped my hands with the handkerchief over my nose, his other hand came from high in the air to under my neck, my knees folded, and I was held backward and downward under the water. All of me. Including my hands that held a once-dry handkerchief. I found myself briefly lying face up as though in a tomb.

As a little girl I had once fallen into an icy fishpond and nearly drowned in the freezing water. I still remember vividly the terrifying sensation of being underwater and fighting for life. I have never completely trusted water since. Under the baptismal waters, that memory flooded back over me, and I recalled Dr. Donaldson's remarks that in baptism we are buried into Christ's death. And I didn't like it there at all. It was death-like there under the baptismal water. Yet I was learning to trust Jesus who died to give us new life.

And I trusted Dr. Donaldson. Immediately he pulled me up out of that death as he pulled me up out of the water, and I felt the water rushing off of me—splashing at first, then dripping down off my wet head, off my eyelashes and the end of my nose and down my shoulders. Dr. Donaldson prayed for me and then turned me around and sent me off out of those baptismal waters cleansed and new.

My soaring spirits were held down only by the weight of one white robe soaked in holy water. I pulled my weight through the water and up the stairs, water splashing everywhere. Someone—who had known me from the time I was little and had watched me grow, even helped me grow in the faith—stood at the top of the stairs with a towel to dry me and a hug to give me as the final touch to my initiation into full membership in the church family.

I dried off, quickly changed out of the white robe into my church clothes, ran a comb through my wet hair, put on the little gold cross my parents had given me to celebrate this special occasion, and slipped into the third pew with family—not quite dry from being baptized, feeling clean and cleansed, with sins big or little all washed off. There I received for the first time the bread and the cup, the very body and blood of the Jesus whom I had just promised to follow. I knew I was God's own. The whole event was incredibly special and very holy, and I began to understand what it means.

I am still learning what it means.

Sometimes I know my mother was right, that I didn't know what baptism meant. But when I claimed Jesus as Lord and Savior, I committed myself to a lifelong process of discovery and to the awesomeness of being a part of the body of Christ. I am still learning.

That's my story. Why do I tell you this now? This is not a time for baptism. That's the stuff of Easter. Or is this Ash Wednesday baptismal sermon just a handy way to kick off the chosen theme for this Lenten season?

No. I talk about baptism on this night because I understand it better than I did when I was twelve. I understand now how soil and water go together. I understand better this night when we smudge our faces with ashes and speak of the need to be penitent because we need to be cleansed.

A prerequisite for authentic cleansing, you see, is authentic dirt, and we've got it. Our soiled foreheads reflect our soiled souls. It's not just that we have bumped up against some ashes on our way out the door. We are broken and sinful and soiled people to the marrow of our bones. It is soil of which we are made and we would be soil yet if God had not scooped us up, dust and all, to breathe God's very own breath into us. The problem is that we do not live as persons filled with the breath of the holy. The good we would do, we do not. That which we would not do, we do with a vengeance. Lord, have mercy on us.

I understand now that it is not just what we as individuals do. It is also our corporate sin—capital-*S* Sin. Racism, oppression, violence, addictions, apathy, selfishness, greed. Structures that make the rich richer and turn the poor into homeless and hopeless people. It is our violating God's creation for personal gain, or worshiping at the feet of false and fake gods. It is our subtle aid to evil, our failure to cooperate with good, for which we must repent. Lord, have mercy on us indeed.

I preach of baptism tonight to start us on our journey and to start us dirty-faced. I hope this journey will, at the end of forty Lenten days, invite us to participate in the death and resurrection of Jesus Christ by reconsidering what our baptism means. We begin a journey soiled, hoping to come to that glorious Easter morning with the sense that, white robed, we have been plunged into the baptismal waters and are emerging sputtering and splashing with new life—with the outpouring of the water of blessing, love, and forgiveness still pouring over us, leaving us dripping wet with God's grace, the smudges on our foreheads washed away. Amen.

*W*oman preacher

Connie Erickson

Connie Erickson is on the pastoral staff at First
Christian Church in Bloomington, Indiana, with
responsibilities in religious education, family
ministries, worship, and pastoral care. She is a
graduate of Defiance College and Christian
Theological Seminary. Her sermon grew out of
reflections, during a retreat, on how
women came to be preachers.

John 4:5–30

She is a Woman Preacher.

To look at her, one would not immediately know it. Her voice
is soft, sometimes like water on a parched soul...sometimes like
water on a honing stone, seeking a sharper edge...more clarity...a
clearer view.

She was not raised to be a Woman Preacher. There were no
Women Preachers in her family. In fact, there were no Women
Preachers as far as anyone knew. There were some Women
Teachers permitted to instruct the very young in religious
things. Her mother said that after her grandfather's retirement, he and her grandmother did serve as custodians for a
congregation for several years. And there was that one time her
mother was part-time treasurer for a brief period when Mr.
Heschel went on vacation. But there were no preachers, only
her.

She was trained to be a Woman Servant. Early years meant
afternoons with all the other women and young girls...days
consumed by daily practice, sewing, cooking, caring for the
young children, tending to the home. Marriage was her highest
hope. She had no intention to set aside the starry-eyed promises
of youth for the call to preach...until that one day she went down

47

to the well...alone, apart from the crowd, in the heat of the day...in the quiet where she could hear herself...be herself...live unto herself....

The dried earth beneath her feet hardened with each step upon it. The sun baked the whole of her being and existence. The stones in the buildings around her hardened. Most persons stayed inside to keep from being scorched by the relentless sun. The cloth she veiled her head with draped out, casting a slight shadow over her eyes, shielding her face from the hardness of the light. Her bodily warmth turned to smoldering sweat as she walked through the streets leading to the well outside the city. It was a normal day, even the heat, just part of the routine.

She arrived at the well and leaned against the stones, reaching to drop the bucket into the cool deep below. The smell of freshness rose as the bucket made its way lower and lower. She heard the splash signaling the discovery of water and waited a few moments. Then she began to pull the rope hand over hand, raising up the filled vessel. She imagined with each pull, the wet taste of cool, fresh water flowing over her lips and renewing her inside.

"May I have a drink?"

A man unknown to her interrupted her safe wellspring. She had not noticed him sitting there. She pretended not to hear; perhaps he would leave her alone. What provoked such an invasion into her quiet?

"I say," he repeated, "give me a drink."

In a moment of forgetfulness, she looked up at the stranger: male, *and* a Jew to boot! "Merciful God!" she protested under her breath, and remembering her manners, she quickly glanced back down at the bucket overflowing with cool refreshment.

He reached out to help her lift the bucket to the edge of the well. She pulled the bucket toward her, continuing to resist his presence.

"Would you mind if I took a cup?" he persisted.

She handed him a cup, and then to both their amazement she blurted out, "How is it that you a Jew ask a drink of me, a woman of Samaria?" She was embarrassed by her unleashed response—were those words from her own mouth? Would that she could grab them back! She groaned inwardly, ashamed. In the silence that fell after her brash inquisition, she offered him a second drink.

She was becoming uncomfortable with their lone presence. *Can't he drink any faster?* she wished...there in the middle of the day, the sun burning brightly...the two of them at the well for all the world to see...the risk of intimacy too great.

He finally set the cup down. *Thank Yahweh!* she thought. *He's finished. I can get my own drink, fill my jar, and get back home, and be rid of this encounter, this well incident once and for all. No one need know....*As she lifted the filled jar to rest upon her head, he dared to speak again.

"If you knew the Gift of Yahweh, and who it is that is saying to you, 'give me a drink,' you would have asked him and he would have given you living water."

Oh, great, she thought, calming the wobbling jar on her head, *one of those traveling mystics. He must have considered me easy prey with none of the menfolk out to bother this time of day.* She was somewhat amused by his speech.

Feeling no longer embarrassed and now less threatened by this vagabond cryptic, she cajoled, "You have no bucket and the well is deep. Where do you get that living water?" There was a teasing air in her reply, "Are you greater than our ancestor Jacob who gave us the well and with his children and flock drank from it?" *Living water,* she thought, *what nonsense! Jacob and his sons are as dead as these stones!*

"Everyone who drinks of this water will be thirsty again."

Well, that's true. She listened. Maybe he's not so crazy after all....

"But those who drink of the water that I will give them will never be thirsty." There was an unusual conviction and authority in his voice. The tone of confidence and assurance, the mystery and power of truth in this foreign word.... "The water I give will become in them a spring of water, gushing up to eternal life."

Her amusement and skepticism turned to curiosity. She took the jar from her head and put it down on the edge of the well. "Sir, give me this water," she mildly demanded, "so that I may never be thirsty!" Thinking about the wild possibility, she added, "or have to keep coming here to draw water!"

He instructed her, "Go call your husband and come back."

What's that *got to do with living water?* she wondered to herself. *Who is this man? That man I live with has never drawn a bucket of water in his life!"*

The stranger was looking straight at her again. His eyes intently focused into her own. *My husband...*she pondered. *My husband...?* she silently questioned. *What difference could it make?* Her words gushed forth, "I have no husband," she replied. "*No* husband."

"You are right!" he beamed. With a smile he went on, "You are right in saying, 'I have no husband,' for you have had five husbands and the one you have now is not your husband." There was an awkward joy in his voice.

It was making her uncomfortable again. Who *is* this man? He was nearly shouting. She worried someone would hear him and observe their meeting. As she turned to look about, he reached his hands forward laying them upon her shoulders.

"What you have said is true!" he exclaimed.

Was this a blessing? She was confused. *He's actually touching me!* she told herself. Was this a pronouncement of her righteousness...a word, a sign truly come from God? What was this feeling flowing in her body? And then, as if out of no will of her own, she spoke, "Sir, I sense that you are a prophet." Staring straight into his eyes she acknowledged, "an angel of God, God's own voice." She had heard it, God's voice, in her own ears and heart.

Here's my chance, she thought, *to ask one of those religious questions that troubles my mind.* In her exuberance, she challenged, "Our ancestors worshiped in this mountain, but you say that the place where people must worship is Jerusalem...." She paused to catch her breath.

Before she could carry on with her own agenda, he interrupted, "Woman, believe me, the hour is coming when you will worship the Father neither on this mountain nor in Jerusalem. You worship what you do not know," he said, dropping his hands from her shoulders to her own hands. Clasping their hands together tightly, he looked at her again with the face of divine glow. "We...," he seemed to be including her, "we worship what we know for salvation is from the Jews. But the hour is coming, and is now here, when true worshipers will worship the Divine in spirit and truth. For the Divine seeks such as these to worship."

Spirit? Truth? She yearned to know his meaning.

"God is spirit," he continued, "and those who worship God must worship in spirit and truth."

What was this man speaking? Were these prophetic words wrapped in mysteries yet to be revealed? The hour is coming...the hour is coming.... His words searched her soul.... Inwardly she wondered, *Maybe that will be the time to make some sense of this man's message!*

"I know," she ventured, "that Messiah is coming, the one called Christ.... When he comes, he will proclaim all things to us...." As she spoke, she noticed a group of people moving toward them.

She pulled her hands from his and reached to pick up her jar. She was anxious to leave before the crowd reached the well, afraid to face their condemning eyes. She turned to go.

As she bid farewell to this prophet, this stranger, he reached out, touching her arm one last time, and spoke, "I am he, the one who is speaking to you."

The Messiah? Could he be, here at Jacob's well...? The words caught in her throat as the people encircled them.

Questions formed on the faces of the crowd. "What do *you* want?" they glared at her. Their posture demanded of him, "Why are *you* speaking with *her*?" No one spoke. Not the disciples. Not the woman at the well. The Messiah did not offer another word. In the silence and truth of the moment, the woman left her water jar and went back into the city.

"Come!" she invited, "Come and see the one who told me everything I have ever done!" The spirit of truth flowed in her speaking, the blessing of God revealed in life, living water.

The people listened to the Woman Preacher. Immediately some people left, going out from the city. They were on their way to Christ.

*M*eticulous mercy is the work of travelers

Rita Nakashima Brock

Rita Nakashima Brock is associate professor in the Endowed Chair in the Humanities at Hamline University, St. Paul, Minnesota. Her book, *Journeys by Heart*, won the Crossroad/Continuum annual award for most outstanding work in women's studies. Rita earned a Ph.D. in philosophy of religion and theology at Claremont Graduate School and has taught at Stephens College and Pacific Lutheran University. She is the immediate past president of Disciples Peace Fellowship. This sermon was delivered at the National Council of Churches Consultation for Racial and Ethnic Women in Ministry.

Luke 8:1-3

The title of your conference, "Women Called to Tell the Idle Tale," comes from the Gospel of Luke, which tells us the most about the female disciples. But why does Luke, who presents many women as preeminent disciples, call their tale "idle" (24:11)? Because "idle" tales were important. Women were the newspapers for communities in which few people could read and in which word spread by the telling of tales. There was no other way for people to know important information about others, about life and birth, about marriage and death, about fortune and misfortune—about the concrete details of life lived in community. The idle tales were crucial to the networks of community and caring that sustain humane life.[1] Luke tells us about the women who traveled with Jesus and told the idle tale. And what can we glean from Luke about the journey of women in the church, especially those of us who choose the work of ministry?

I imagine the women in Luke's story—Mary, Joanna, Susanna, and many others—looking much like you. At the crossroads of Asia and Africa, they would have had light olive to black skins, a few with pale skin, but not many. They would have had black or brown hair and dark, rich-looking eyes. I have to say, standing up here and looking at you, that you are a sight for sore eyes. I cherish this opportunity tonight to stand before my sisters of color, to see your beautiful faces, to hear your wonderful, strong voices, and to speak words of hope and empowerment to those of you who are close to my heart.

There they were, these women—Mary of Magdala, Joanna, Susanna, and many others. They found themselves on a journey, traveling with others who had experienced a new wholeness—freed of many demons and healed of infirmities, Luke tells us. They had also been enticed by Jesus' vision of liberation and wholeness—a vision first proclaimed, by the way, by Mary, Jesus' mother.

The women had joined this carpenter/rabbi from Nazareth in his proclamation of the vision and in the exorcising of demons and healing of the broken that were marks of that vision. These were women who knew the power of being freed from inner demons. Luke does not tell us what those demons were, but I think we probably have some idea, don't we?

There were demons inside those women's heads that said, "Women can't do this; we don't just drop everything and start ministering to people in public. You have to let a man do this. No woman has ever done this before. No one will pay attention to you if you try."

Other demons said, "Your husband is more important than you. Your job in life is to be his servant, to make him feel better, to love him faithfully no matter what happens. It doesn't matter that he beats you and forces you to do what you don't want. Your only life is with him."

A few leftover demons from childhood might have carried images of the uncle who molested, of the parent who left bruises and broken bones or who ignored us completely, of the teacher who made us feel stupid. We carry these demons from the past like the faint images on a scratched, dim mirror. They haunt our lives as lingering sitting ghosts, determined to squeeze the life out of us.

I carried some of these demons myself, including having learned to confuse abuse with love and feeling stupid in school. And I remember other demons too, demons that made me ashamed of who I am. My hair was not blond and my eyes were too dark. I was too short and too skinny. When I was little, I spoke with an accent, so my English was bad. No matter what my education and success, in this society, I am always a stranger.

I came here from Japan with my mother and white stepfather when I was six. (My birth father is Puerto Rican, but that's too long a story to tell here.) I had to change languages and cultures. In the twenty-three years that I have lived in this country, in all the years I have struggled to adapt and to fit in as best I could, I have always been aware that I was an outsider. Still, people look at me and ask what country I am from, which happens also to my Nisei and Sansei friends. White Americans often assume that anyone who is not white or black is only here temporarily. And I think they wish blacks would go away too. On forms that ask for racial identities, the directions always say, "check one." I am *three*—Japanese, Puerto Rican, and Taino Indian. In this society, only one race counts, and all of mine are the wrong ones.

My Asian sisters with eyes shaped like sideways teardrops talk about wanting big eyes and my black sisters with hair as springy and soft as woodland moss discuss wanting "good" hair. These demons ask us to objectify our bodies, hate them, struggle with them as if they were our enemies, starving them, bleaching them, and numbing them with drugs or alcohol. We grow up in a culture deeply uncomfortable with the physical. It asks us to deny all that makes us distinctively ourselves. Deeply isolated from intimacy, we spend years in lonely prisons behind bars of alienation and self-hate.

We are told that Mary had seven demons cast out of her. I think most of us, when we are honest about our experiences as women of color in this racist, classist, homophobic, and sexist society, can probably name seven demons we have battled. I do not know how to grow up as sensitive, caring, connected persons in any society without having deeply internalized the ghosts and demons of that society. Your presence here today is testimony to your own struggle with casting out demons and your commitment to empowering others to defeat their own demons.

With the liberation of their demons, the women—Mary, Joanna, Susanna, and many others—had found with the Jesus community a new life, moving in and toward liberation and wholeness. According to Luke, the women disciples had been healed of evil spirits and infirmities, traveled with Jesus and the men, and provided for the community out of their own resources.

Here they were, that group of travelers, who look much like you, taking on that long journey. The hope deep in their hearts bubbled up along the weary miles. I can hear the intense theological discussions they had with each other about the meaning of their lives. I can see the friendship and support they gave each other for their survival. In long discussions with Jesus, they worked out the concrete implications of the visions he proclaimed, both learning from him and teaching him how he must regard and treat women. For we know he both taught and listened to women. Imaging the growing mutuality of that time together, the depth of love that grew like an enormous tree, reaching way down into the earth, grounded in the energy of life itself, and towering into the heavens, soaring high into the clear air of a new reality. And the hope, like a chrysalis that has just begun to crack open, setting free the delicate, beautiful, winged creature inside.

They cradled that hope everywhere, walking in their dusty, sandaled feet, wrapped in some well-worn homespun to keep out the chill of desert nights, long miles in front of them, voices hoarse after proclaiming so much, and always the danger of being caught alone, of the robbers and rapists lurking in the shadows. Having been women of some means, at least some of them, this hardship must have been quite a trial. As if that weren't enough, they also had to endure those dense male disciples who resented their presence and told them they were not equal to them. You know those guys; they kept arguing about who was number one and trying to shove out the competition.

The discomfort and danger notwithstanding, what the women created and found on that journey was worth the risks. We know it was worth the risks because their journey is our journey. With the casting out of seven demons, we discover that their journey and our journey take on seven angels.

I call the first angel *subtlety*, the capacity to listen to soft, faint voices. Few women get thunderous invitations to become ministers. While we hear of the call of some of the male disciples, we have no record that the women received a direct call to join Jesus.

In 1978, when the Pacific and Asian Center for Theology and Strategies in Berkeley called the first-ever consultation for Asian and Pacific American women in ministry, I remember our descriptions of being called to ministry. Few of us felt a dramatic turnaround and sudden need to be ordained; most of us described a slow awakening. Because many of us had never known another Asian woman minister, the idea that this was something we could do came gradually with a deepening of self-confidence and faith. With active resistance sometimes around us or just the absence of support and role models in our communities, there was no dramatic moment of assurance, no thunderous certainty. Just swirls of self-doubt and hope, of fear and courage, of stubborn persistence in the face of many counterforces, and, finally, the slow birth of insight and inspiration.

Maybe the lack of support has changed for those of you who are younger. But if my experiences at the women's interseminary conference in April are any indication, many women in ministry experience the same thunderous silence of the call to women we find in Luke. Our call to ministry is subtle, a dawning comprehension that emerges as we work in the church and as we find our legs standing on shifting ground.

But rest assured, however long it takes, the Holy Spirit is persistent in her gentle calling. This subtlety of ours is a profound gift. It helps us understand self-doubt, as well as the historical invisibility of powerful and competent women. This same subtlety is what attunes us to looking below the surface of biblical texts for hints of the work of women who have been virtually erased by the tradition. Subtlety empowered the women in Luke to notice the lame, hungry child tucked away in the shadows of that doorway and give her bread, to hear the strain in Jesus' voice at the end of a long day and take him away from the crowds, to notice the first flush of fever on a face and offer cool water, to detect the note of despair behind a cheerful greeting and offer a comforting touch. This subtlety, we know, is a powerful thing.

The second angel is one I mentioned earlier, the angel of holistic *liberation*, of being exorcised of our demons and restored to moments of wholeness in our lives. The infirmities of our lives no longer get in our way, but are sources of strength. If we have not dealt with our own demons, we will not be able to help others to see their own, for we cannot guide others to where we have not been. With the exorcism of our demons and the healing of our bodies, psyches, and spirits, we become reconciled to our bodies with a sense of solicitous care and profound appreciation for the miracle of being embodied, of the joys of incarnation—of being in the flesh—in all its myriad, differently abled forms and colors.

Luke says that the women provided for the travelers out of their own resource. This is the third angel of the women's journey—*generosity*. For some of us, resources mean money and time, the obvious things to share. And these obvious things are crucial. The community of God requires that the poor and downtrodden be housed, fed, clothed, healed, and educated. But what did the women share who had few material resources and who worked long and hard to get by? As Katie Cannon says, "Who make somethin' out of nothin'?"

At that consultation for Asian and Pacific women in ministry in 1978, I remember one of the most powerful moments was the time we told our stories to each other and shared our searches for a home in a world that marginalized us at every turn. For Asian and Pacific Americans, this is a struggle with invisibility. At that consultation, we talked of feeling like homeless people, nomads in an inhospitable land. We talked also of feeling, with the other women, *finally*, a sense of home, of being with others who understood our struggles, our cultural codes and language, our commitment to the church. In our journey together for a few short days, we created home for each other by the honest and open sharing of our struggles, fears, and hopes. We gave each other our vulnerability. We shared in physical ways, too, by cooking together and sharing the food from our various cultures. Our gathering, all of us together, is this third angel of the women's journey—generosity, which is the basis of mutuality and community.

In creating home for the journey, the women in Luke did not just focus on their own well-being, but they worked together with the fourth angel in their journey together. This angel is *activism* empowered by compassion and courage. Seventy disciples were anointed to go out and heal the sick, exorcise demons, and preach the vision of the *basileia*. Women were among the disciples, according to Luke, so we can assume that some of those seventy were Mary, Joanna, Susanna, and the many others. To minister to people and to preach a radically egalitarian vision of life in the community of God was no small act of political subversion under the shadow of Rome.

Still today, for many women in ministry, to work for and preach the equality of women in a male-dominant society, to seek the ending of poverty in an exploitative capitalist state, to join the liberation struggle of all people of color in a racist society—to cry out for global justice—involves huge risks, including exclusion from the company of other ministers, the loss of our pulpits, or the absence of churches willing to call us. And here we are, doing it anyway.

The fifth angel of the women's journey is not so easy to talk about. It is *failure*. This is not what we like to hear. We want heroines who make no mistakes, women we can idealize from the past, to whom we can point as having done it all right. But the disciples fell asleep in Gethsemane. Luke tells us they all did, not just the men. This journey of ours involves moments of remorse, of regret for what we have not done and should have, of fear and retreat when our actions ought to emerge from our profoundest visions. We live sometimes with regret and grief. Perhaps you have never faced such a moment of reckoning, but I know I have, and they are important moments of growth for me. It is important for us to know our own failures and accept our limitations.

The sixth angel, and one that appears as an undertone behind all the other marks, is *meticulous mercy*. My friend and womanist poet Angela Jackson talks about this in her poem "The Love of Travelers." She describes a journey with two friends. At a rest stop on the way to Mississippi, they find a fluttering butterfly mired in an oil slick. One of them "tender in the fingertips" tries to wipe its wings free, but the oil smears like lipstick "under the method of her mercy for something so slight and graceful, injured, beyond the love of travelers." The body ruptured from its wings as it lifted itself between the washed wings. "Imagine," says Angela, "the agony of a self separated by gentlest repair." None of them has the nerve to kill it, though they know they should.

> We walked away, the last of the oil welding the
>   butterfly
> to the wood of the picnic table.
> The wings stuck out and quivered when wind went by.
> Whoever found it must have marveled at this.
> And loved it for what it was and
> had been.
> I think, meticulous mercy is the work of travelers,
> and leaving things as they are punishment or reward.
> I have died for the smallest things.
> Nothing washes off.[2]

Meticulous mercy appears at the most crucial moment of failure for the entire community. Like that butterfly stuck in oil, Jesus is impaled on a cross, slowly dying as the women watch helplessly, powerless to save him yet drawn to him in his suffering. They watch helplessly his agony. Perhaps one of them, tender in the fingertips, walked over to a Roman soldier and quietly spoke to him, placing a gold coin in his hand so that he would end the pain with a spear in Jesus' side.

In the midst of their helplessness and fear, their meticulous mercy empowers their persistent presence, their courage in not running away. In their traveler's love, they watch in profound sorrow and grief. We know this kind of mercy, the punishment and reward of accepting things as they are. Their community is like the body of that butterfly ripped from its mired wings of hope. This death would not wash off.

Meticulous mercy appears when a mother waits all night for her child's fever to break. A woman spends months at the side of her husband dying of cancer. A grandmother walks her grandson to school past drug dealers and abandoned buildings. A daughter tends to aging parents, watching as they fade into infancy and death. A group of women meticulously prepares their dead brother for his journey on the ghost road.

My own mother had cancer for eleven years. At the end, she had lost half her face to surgeries and lived in a disfigured, ravaged body. When she slipped into a coma, I remember sitting by her bed and holding her hand. I told her I knew she was ready to go and I tried to pull her spirit from her. I imagined it leaving her through our clasped hands and flowing into me. The next day, she drew her last breath. Meticulous mercy, most tender and most compassionate, can end in grief and sorrow, and our grieving itself is born of that mercy.

The last angel comes because nothing washes off. We remember. The women's journey is born of that meticulous mercy that refused to desert Jesus, that mourned his passing with intense grief, and that refused to let the Roman execution destroy their community. The last angel is *vision.*

I am not talking about vision that is a nice fantasy story or abstract hope. I mean real vision—the kind that comes after serious fasting and physical trial, an opening of one's heart to the spirit, that catches us unaware when we are buried in our deepest grief. It wells up from deep inside, from the very depths of our being. That kind of vision can sear our sorrow and make us cry out in joy, the ecstasy of giving ourselves over to our dreams, our deepest sorrows and highest hopes. Some of you come from cultures that understand vision better, cultures that encourage vision quests, and that know how to prepare people for such visions.

And what vision was born of the sorrow of meticulous mercy? We know, don't we? A vision only possible to those who could accept their own limits, their helplessness, fear, and grief, and still stay to the bitter end. Mary, Joanna, and Susanna stayed all the way through to the end and, in their grief, returned to Jesus' grave. Why? Because they could not let it go, they would not let it go. The experiences of their journey, the liberation, the wholeness, the mutuality, the intense theological thinking, the caring, the solidarity—all of it was real. And they were not willing to have this Roman execution destroy it, wash it away. So they returned and their meticulous mercy reaped the idle tale, the tale, as travelers, we continue to tell, our work as travelers.

Let the angels of subtlety, liberation, generosity, activism, failure, mercy, and vision carry you on their wings of hope to the end of all our days as you go, my sisters, telling the idle tale. Tell it often, tell it passionately, and tell it well. Amen and amen. Let the people say amen.

---

[1]My thanks to Fred Craddock for providing me this background information about the meaning of "idle tales."

[2]Angela Jackson, "The Love of Travelers." Quoted by permission of the poet. (The complete poem can be found in *The Pushcart Prize XIV: Best of the Small Presses, 1989-90*, edited by Bill Henderson. Pushcart Press, 1989.)

*D*o you want to be healed?

Carolyn Bullard-Zerweck

Carolyn Bullard-Zerweck serves as the North Texas Area representative for Church World Service—CROP, in Dallas, Texas. She is a graduate of Abilene Christian College and Brite Divinity School. Married to a minister, and the mother of three, Carolyn is currently in training at the Pastoral Counseling and Education Center in Dallas, working toward AAPC certification.

John 5:1–9

A long and complicated journey has brought me from the Church of Christ and Abilene Christian College to Brite Divinity School and to this pulpit. It is not my intention to share with you the details of my journey in faith. But perspective shapes meaning. Where I've been is part of who I am and who I am shapes the message that I bring.

I looked over my years at Brite, and at the changes in my theology and in my understanding of life. Sometimes I wish I knew *for sure* as much about God as I did when I started. My years here have been full of change and growth, and sometimes I feel like Alice in *Alice in Wonderland* when the caterpillar asked her, "Who are you?" and she replied, "I know who I was when I woke up this morning but I think I must have changed several times since then."

This scripture reading from the Gospel of John has had particular meaning for me in the past few years. We see with the mind's eye a picture of crowds of very sick people: handicapped, blind, lame, paralyzed, masses of diseases and afflicted humanity waiting near the pool for a chance to be cured, hoping for a miracle—praying that *this time* they will be the one to be healed.

One of these is a man who had been sick for *thirty-eight* years. Jesus saw this man and asked him what appears on the surface to be an incredibly harsh, even cruel, question: "Do you want to be healed?" Man, do you want to get well? My first, instinctive reply is, "Well, *of course* he wants to get well. He's been sick for thirty-eight years—living by the pool, but he doesn't have anyone to help him into the pool. Someone else *always* beats him to it. *Of course* he wants to be healed!"

And, I wonder, why couldn't Jesus have just gone ahead and healed the man? He was going to heal him anyway. Why ask such a question? But then I imagine that for the rest of his life, that man would remember the day of his recovery, and every time he thought of it, he would hear Jesus asking him, "Do you want to be healed?"

The answer may appear to be obvious, but often what we *think* we want and what we *say* we want are *not* what we really want.

Maybe life was pretty comfortable on the porches of Beth-zatha, maybe there was some benefit in staying the way he was. Oh, it may have not been ideal, but he had lived that way so long. Healing would mean a change in lifestyle, he would have to do some things he was not accustomed to doing. Did he *want* to be healed?

This question has particular application for our day—for the brokenness of a world in which terrorism continually rears its ugly head, a world in which apartheid is allowed to exist, a world in which sexism, racism, and nationalism are either blatantly expressed or subtly masked. On a smaller scale, in our own personal lives, we may be avoiding healing through our striving for money, for success, for power, and through our constant endless activity.

And so we go to the pool and sit *just* close enough to the healing waters to convince ourselves that what we *really* want is healing—but not close enough to do us any good. Yes, God is the source of healing, and healing, like grace, is a gift. But it is not a gift that will be thrust on us unawares—against our will. Healing, like any gift, must be accepted, must in some way be desired. And, like grace, it is not cheap. It may be free, but it will demand *something* of us.

That "something" is often the very thing we don't want to give up. Seward Hiltner calls this, in psychological terminology, "secondary gains." In other words, we may be getting some kind of benefit out of our sickness, whether it be not taking responsibility for our actions, blaming others, blaming God. We may be saying, "Well, that's just the way it is, that's reality—so I can stay depressed or angry or continue feeling guilty, because it is easier and *so much more* comfortable than having to change."

What new challenges must we face? What will be asked of us if we are healed? The question has implications for each of us as individuals and also as part of the community.

As an individual, what does it mean to be healed? There is no one formula, no one answer, no one solution that can be applied to every life so that we can say, "There, this is what you do and everything will be fine!" Those kinds of answers tend to be Band-Aids. The answer must be worked out in intimate relationship with God, in our own individual personalities and circumstances, and also in relationship with the community.

Healing our broken world, both internally and externally, takes many forms. Sometimes we don't even recognize healing. We don't know what it looks like. Our definitions are distorted by the definitions of the world around us.

Greg Davis is a student at Brite Divinity School. I was in classes with Greg for about four years. But I never paid much attention to Greg. He's quiet, unobtrusive. I would describe him much like Clark Kent, "a mild-mannered young reporter from the Daily Planet." But this past year Greg made a courageous stand for peace and justice. He became a volunteer for Witness for Peace in Nicaragua, where he is now.

Greg and I had a class together last fall. One morning we both arrived outside the classroom at the same time. I asked him if the class before ours had dismissed. He said he didn't know. I asked if he had checked by opening the door. He said, no, he wouldn't do that because some professors got really angry and one had even thrown a book at him. "Well," I said, "I am not afraid." And I boldly opened the door to discover...an empty room.

We went in and put our books down. I was inwardly congratulating myself on *my* assertiveness and *my* lack of fear, when it suddenly hit me. I turned to Greg and I said, "But *you* are going to Nicaragua! I can open doors all day long. But *I* can't go to Nicaragua!"

The courage it takes to heal our world doesn't always look as we think it should. Healing our world doesn't require *all* of us to go to Nicaragua, but it does require *some* of us to go.

Healing may mean life-shattering change, for some. It may mean facing the truth about one's life, and then facing the consequences of that truth.

By saying, "Yes, I want to be healed," we have to look into ourselves, into the brokenness of our lives. We may have to get *angry* in order to heal, or maybe healing will mean screaming, or crying, or laughing, or dancing, or singing.

Or healing may mean the acceptance of some reality. It may mean forgiving oneself, letting go of past mistakes. We may need to release ourselves from the cycle of paralyzing guilt. In this cycle, we know we are *not* perfect, and so we try harder and harder to *be* perfect, and to *do* everything and to do it perfectly. In this instance, healing may mean the acceptance of our humanness, our limitedness, and giving up trying to be God.

Healing may be forgiving others, letting go of blame and old grievances, past hurts.

Healing means opening our hearts to allow God's healing love to flow in. It does not mean that there will *be* no more brokenness. The healing process is never complete. But healing is to be found in relationship with God.

However, we cannot be healed alone. Healing, for the community of faith, is a process—a struggle. We either win together or we all lose together. There is no grabbing of God's grace and running back to our side and yelling, "Nyah, nyah— I'm healed and you're not!"

On an ABC summer special about women in the 1980s, Peter Jennings concluded that "when women are stronger, we will all be stronger." Insert any name in the place of women: blacks, Hispanics, handicapped, elderly, children, men. We don't get strong on someone else's weakness.

It is an oversimplification to say that there are two kinds of people. But I find Walter Brueggemann's writing to be helpful here to illustrate my point. Brueggemann describes two polarities of theology in the Hebrew Scripture—structure legitimation, and embrace of pain. Briefly, structure legitimation is the voice of those who want to maintain the status quo, the upholders of the institution, the powers that be, the "haves" of this world. The embrace of pain is the voice of the oppressed, the voice of the marginalized, the disenfranchised, the "have nots."[1]

Brueggemann's thesis is that faith is worked out in maintaining the tension between the two poles. Faith comes in not going too far one way or the other, but in staying in the tension between the two. In applying this model to the text, healing also comes in working out the tension between the two.

Professor Toni Craven explained in her "Introduction to Hebrew Scriptures" course at Brite that if all we do is structure legitimation, if our whole lives are focused on maintaining the status quo, upholding the institution, then there is a pain we are blocking—something we're ignoring, something we don't want to look at or deal with. But, she says, the other side of this is: If all we are doing is embracing the pain, what we *really* want is structure legitimation.

Do the powers that be, the upholders of the institution, the maintainers of the status quo, want to be healed? In order to do so, they—we—must face the pain we do not wish to see.

And do the political and social activists, the feminists, the liberationists, want to be healed? In order for that to happen, they—we—must be willing to move beyond our pain, toward healing, and admit that, yes, what we really want is to be legitimated by the institution.

Now, this is *not* particularly comforting to me personally. In the words of a former Brite student, Larry Crocker, "I'd rather be mad!" And I'm so *good* at being mad!

As irritating as it is to me, I cannot be healed in isolation, I cannot be healed without the sexist people of this world. I cannot be healed without the racist people of this world. Healing—wholeness—comes in the process of working together. *Either we all win together or we all lose together.*

The process of healing is both an individual and a communal one. It is not enough for the individual to be healed because we are in relationship with one another.

Doug Stenberg is 15 years old, the son of Loren and Nancy Stenberg, friends of ours in Richardson. Doug was a teen helper at vacation Bible school last summer—an active, energetic, athletic young man. Last July, while Doug and his father were surfing in California, Doug was thrown by a wave and was left paralyzed from the waist down.

Doug has undergone therapy at Dallas Rehabilitation Center. His father remarks that Doug's spirit is exceptionally strong; in fact, it is Doug's spirit that has helped to pull his family through the crisis. Doug wants to be better and he believes that he will be better. But healing for Doug may not mean that he will ever walk again.

Doug's story pushes me to a new understanding of healing. His healing is taking place in the context of family and friends. As they work together to help, Doug's healing becomes a reality for all of them. His father said, "Somehow we have to go on living. Somehow we have to find a sense of normalcy, *whatever* that means in this situation."

That's how I see healing: seeking to be whole in the situations that we are given—not perfect, not rigid, but whole, full of the life God gives us.

Healing comes in intimate relationship with God. And the answer, the next step, will be worked out in that relationship. God is everywhere and always calling us into relationship. God is always calling us to wholeness, to healing.

Do we want to be healed?

---

[1]Walter Brueggemann, "A Shape for Old Testament Theology, I: Structure Legitimation." *The Catholic Biblical Quarterly,* 47 (1985), pp. 28–46; and "A Shape for Old Testament Theology, II: Embrace of Pain," *The Catholic Biblical Quarterly*, 47 (1985), pp. 395–415.

$\mathcal{T}$he transfiguration

Becky A. Hebert

Becky Hebert is pastor of Lake Herriot
Christian Church in Minneapolis, Minnesota. A
graduate of Texas Christian University and Brite
Divinity School, she served previously on the staff
of Park Avenue Christian Church in New York
City. Becky is the mother of two grown daughters
and worked in interior design prior to
her move into ministry.

Mark 9:2–8

I don't know when it happened—when it slipped away from
me. I must have been too busy to notice, until one day in a
conversation with a student at Austin College where I was
serving as a chaplain intern. That day, I knew, I no longer had
the close relationship with Jesus to which she was referring.
There was a story that used to circulate around seminary about
a young man who went off to seminary being warned that he
shouldn't go to this evil place, because there he might lose Jesus.
The story was meant to be funny. I failed to see the humor in it any
longer. The Gospel reading of today caught my attention. The
ending words, "no one with them any more, but only Jesus" (Mark
9:8b), echoed in my mind. I was still up on the mountain standing
in the presence of Elijah, Moses, and God. Jesus was nowhere
to be found. I had lost him. Had all the Old Testament courses I'd
chosen to take in seminary changed me? I could relate to Moses,
the prophets, and the psalmists in their relationship to God.
But Jesus was gone. Oh, I wanted him back. So off I went to read
this scripture and struggle with it in order to develop a sermon, in
hopes that in my struggle I would be led back to Christ.

In the quiet of the afternoon, I curled up in bed with my Bible
and slowly read the words of Mark, trying to understand my

painful separation. Then suddenly there it was: a vision—or call it a scene—running through my mind, of an event from summer.

There I was in Louisiana at the foot of my father's grave. His name, Traville Lawrence Hebert, loomed out at me. And I cried. I had known all that summer that I might find myself forced to return to the site of my father's grave after twenty-one years. My Uncle Buddy was dying of cancer—an uncle I loved dearly. To say good-bye to him was going to be painful. It also meant reopening a past I had avoided for years. I was twenty-one years old when my father died. I had not been able to bring myself back to visit his grave since. My uncle's graveside service would be in that same graveyard.

The day came. The phone rang. It was Mama. "Uncle Buddy has died." I must have not answered for she spoke again, "Becky, we are going to the funeral, aren't we? If so, plans need to be made. When do you want to leave?" We agreed on a time, and I began to busy myself with making reservations, canceling other plans, and finding someone to feed the dog. I called Rachel, my daughter, at work. She had said she wouldn't go to the funeral. She was angry with me for not finding time to take her to see her uncle before he died. She answered the phone. "Rachel, I just got a call from Grandma. Uncle Buddy has died. Do you want to go to the funeral?"

"Yes, I want to go."

I was so pleased. I wanted her to be with me. I had more than Uncle Buddy back home to bid good-bye.

The next two days unfolded in the midst of aunts, uncles, cousins, and old friends. They had all gotten so old over the years. Roger's son looked like the Roger I remembered. There I stood in the past made present.

We all filed out together in cars, first to the church and then to the graveyard. The walk from the car to the grave site seemed so long. Mother went off to sit with her brothers and sisters. Rachel and I got separated from each other in the crowd. And I stood alone—very alone.

The service began—led by Masons. Masons? My beloved uncle had been a Mason? My father had been a Mason, an organization that withheld membership from blacks. I had trouble all weekend relating to these people, the people of my childhood. I loved these people, but I no longer understood them, nor they me. They were having as much trouble relating to me, a future minister with radical views, as I to them. I grieved the distance. I grieved my many losses. And I saw my father's grave in the distance. The service was over. I walked in the direction of his grave. Tears poured out of my eyes. There he was. A man I loved dearly. Would he understand me today?

My mother and my aunt walked up and wrapped their arms around me. Aunt Ara said, "Becky, I loved him too." We cried together. And then my mother, who had never been able to understand what I was doing in seminary (she usually told her friends that she thought I planned to do religious education or counseling or something like that—but she had never been able to see her daughter as a minister), said, "Becky, when I die, will you do my funeral?" She saw me as a minister. "Oh, mother, you ask too much of me," was all that I could answer.

The vision passed. I lay curled up in bed with my Bible, more perplexed than when I had begun. What does any of this have to do with this scripture—a vision of death intermingled with my identity as a minister? I was confused. I reread the scripture. I reflected on it.

Jesus takes Peter, James, and John up this high mountain—away from the crowd, away from the other disciples, so they can be alone. They climb the mountain. And strange things begin to happen. Jesus, their friend, changes before their eyes, becomes a sort of ghost-like figure. Two more ghosts, Elijah and Moses, appear on the scene. They stand around chit-chatting with each other. Peter is terrified. I would be too, wouldn't you? Peter mumbles something about making three booths for them. After all, what does one say to ghosts? To make matters worse, a cloud casts a shadow over them, and a voice comes out of the cloud, "This is my beloved Son, listen to him." Suddenly, the heavenly visitors vanish. The three disciples take a quick look around but do not see anyone. Jesus only is there with them.

Are Peter, James, and John being asked to let go of a past? Elijah and Moses—perhaps they are representatives of the great religious figures of Israel's past.

That must be it, I thought. The vision and the scriptures came together. But it didn't bring Jesus back. I had lived through the heartache of saying good-bye to my past. But it had not brought Jesus back.

I closed my Bible and put it away. Enough! I was in no mood to struggle any more.

Yet, it would not leave me alone. Every lecture I heard in the days ahead, every conversation, every book I read, I found myself searching for the missing piece. It had to be there.

And then, in the quiet of a worship service one day, I listened to a sermon. And I knew. I knew! And I couldn't wait to get home. I had to write it down. I had to capture it, for I knew.

One is not scared in the presence of God. To stand in God's presence brings only peace, a sense of wholeness and oneness with the universe. So why were Peter, James, and John scared?

They were taken up a mountain to watch the transfiguration of Jesus. The disciples were led into the unfolding mystery of their teacher's greatness. They were shown the fate of messiahship, not only for Jesus but for all who would be his followers. One cannot watch the transfiguration of Jesus without being transformed. And that, my friends, is a scary reality— a fear that can easily blind one into losing sight of their fate. "Jesus, it is good that we are here; we will learn to build houses of worship for you. Three if you like, one for you and one for Moses and one for Elijah. We will work hard at filling them to capacity. We will even plan some nice programs to attract the folk—some dinner parties, and enlightened Bible study courses, plays, good sermons, good music...."

"Not what you had in mind, huh, God? Not programs planned for the purpose of filling shrines built to your honor? You don't want transformed buildings but transformed people? You want programs that will lead them into the unfolding mystery of the greatness of which they are called to be participants?"

God has brought us here to see the transfiguration of Jesus, to be transformed, and to become transformers.

My relationship with Jesus was not and is not lost. It has been radically changed. Where I end and Christ begins is hard to discern anymore. One doesn't walk down a mountain after an experience of transformation and relate in the same way. I am being transfigured into the likeness of Christ. You are here to be transformed into the likeness of Christ. This greatness that is happening to me and to you is hard to admit and accept, and even harder to live out.

On July 8, 1986, exactly one year after Uncle Buddy's death, my mother died suddenly of heart failure. I felt as if I had been stripped of all earthly backups. I was an orphan. I could no longer retreat to the soft warmth of motherly protection. I was left to walk the tight rope of life and my net had been plucked out from under me. I was alone, and I wanted to go home.

I was alone, alone but left with the gift she had given me, an awareness of my identity with Christ. "No one with them any more, but only Jesus." Peter, James, and John saw that day on the mountain a vision of death and resurrection, the fate of messiahship—not only for Jesus, but for all who would be his followers.

Life is a never-ending cycle of journeys up the mountain and down the mountain to the cross—of being caught up in transforming experiences of death and resurrection...of standing at the foot of your father and mother's grave to claim your identity of "Christ/likeness."

$\mathcal{W}$hy are you afraid?

Diane Caughron

Diane Caughron is pastor of the Bowling
Green–New Harmony Pastoral Unity, Bowling
Green, Missouri. She has degrees from Lynchburg
College, the University of Illinois, and Brite
Divinity School. Before entering the ministry,
Diane taught high school English and served as a
school, public, and college librarian.

Matthew 8:23–27

Much of the Bible is a series of little vignettes. We get a lot of one-scene episodes. They don't give the whole picture, not by a long shot. They don't even give the whole story of an event, much less of what happened around that scene, or the result of it, or much discussion of it. It's rather like slides of your vacation. They don't show the whole thing!

We are left with the job of interpretation of such scenes. And it is almost impossible—or at least very difficult. It's no wonder there are so many opinions and interpretations of the scriptures! And so many times we hear only superficial interpretations of so many of Jesus' sayings and episodes, especially of his miracles. We get the little vignette, and we don't know what to do with it.

This episode recorded in Matthew is a perfect example. It is a familiar passage, a familiar scene in Jesus' life. His disciples got into a boat with him to go over to the other side of the sea, and no sooner were they off than he fell asleep. So when the storm arose and increased to a dangerous intensity, they became afraid. It must really have been quite a storm, for some of these guys were used to boats and had even grown up in them, fishing for a living since their youth. But they were afraid and woke Jesus up. We assume his comment to them was a rebuke: "Why are you afraid, you of little faith?" (Matthew 8:26). And he calmly stilled the storm.

We assume he scolded them for their fear, for not having enough faith. But somehow that simple interpretation here bothers me. I don't think that's all there is to it at all. I think we may be missing the whole point of the story if we drop it there. Jesus simply had more depth and understanding than that. If we are willing to grapple with the story a bit, we might just be able to dig a little deeper and gain much more insight and more spiritual depth from this incident.

Too often a quick interpretation only provides us with an "easy answer." And those easy answers can disturb us deeply. They may lead people to feel guilt or to reject Jesus' message because they cannot live up to it.

The easy answer here is that if we really believe in Jesus, we will never be afraid of anything. If we really have faith, we will have no fear! The scolding he gave the disciples would also apply to us!

But things are not really that easy. They are not nearly that cut-and-dried, and Jesus knew it too. There's something more here than that easy interpretation.

Yet, when we read about this event, we picture it simply as something that happened, very simply and plainly, and that's all there is to it. What we see is what we get! They wake Jesus; he scolds them for their fear; he stills the storm; and that is that. So be it. Amen. They get to the other shore and the whole thing is forgotten.

Well, I doubt that. People just don't live like that! They talk about things. I imagine that Jesus and the disciples spent a lot of time talking about that storm and the roots of their fear, as well as the fears that were yet to come in the storms of their lives and the storms of their faith.

In fact, I don't think Jesus was scolding them at all. I think he was asking them a question to make them think: "Why are you afraid?"

Jesus knew that they needed to be in touch with their fears, with what their fears made them do. He wanted them to think about how their fears made them act or react—or *not* act or react!

Jesus probably spent much time after that incident helping his disciples learn how to control and use their fear, rather than letting their fear control them. He wanted them to get on top of their fears, or they surely would be sunk!

If there was any scolding, it was because the disciples were letting their fear control them. They were not using their fear to direct their salvation.

Picture them in that boat with the gale at full force. Several are hanging on for dear life. A couple of them crouch in the bottom of the boat. Maybe two of them are trying to bring the sails down, and perhaps one is frantically trying to bail the water out of the boat. Somehow they manage to wake up Jesus.

Now, before you laugh at them, put yourself in that boat! Where would you be? I think I'd be hanging on for dear life. I've seen sudden storms move in before, with lightning and thunder flashing and booming and wind gusting, swirling trees as if they were made of rope. I can imagine what they would do to a boat out on a sea! I know how afraid I feel even when I am safe in a house during a violent storm, especially if there are tornado warnings!

So if I have faith, does that mean I should not be afraid during such a storm? Of course it doesn't. It does mean I need to be in touch with that fear, to be able to question it and be able to control it. I use the fear to direct my acts toward safety, rather than letting it immobilize me—which might put me in more danger than if I acted wisely. To think that because I believe I do not have to fear could be a grave mistake. Better to act wisely and put myself in a safe place.

So it was with the disciples. Knowing their fear and gaining control of it, would enable all of them to do the things that needed to be done to maximize their chances of survival in that boat. They needed to let down the sails, bail the water, distribute their weight. They had to be alert to changes or things that happened that demanded action for their safety, rather than just hanging on for dear life!

"Why are you afraid?" It is a significant question addressed to the disciples, one they probably had to wrestle with long and hard. (It did stick long enough to make it into the gospel!)

"Why are you afraid?" Are you afraid the boat is going to sink and you will be swallowed up in the sea? What is the worst that could happen? What are the chances of it happening? What can you *do* about it? Can you prevent it? Are you worried about only yourself or also about your companions? What can you do to help them? Sometimes in helping others, we forget our own fear. Sometimes if we stick together and do things together, we forget our fear.

What would you have done if I had not been there? Does it make any difference that I was there? (What questions those would be for Jesus to ask!) What will you do with your fear when it comes again?

Can't you hear him, later on, when they came to arrest him, and he turned to his disciples and asked, "Why are you afraid? Do you think you will be arrested too? What if you are? And what if you aren't? What can you do? What do you think is expected of you? How can you control your fear to let it work for you and for me?"

Of course, the disciples didn't conquer it right then. It would take years. But later, when they remembered his words, his teachings, their long conversations, this question would shine through to direct their struggle with fear. One day most of them *would* be arrested, but by then they would have learned to conquer their fear. They would learn how to let fear take a back seat to duty. They would learn how to use their fear to give them energy for accomplishing things for Christ in spite of opposition. They would learn how to work through their fear and turn it into strength.

It is the same thing we all need to learn. We must get in touch with our fears and face them. We must name them and learn how to control them. Fear can be a paralyzing thing. When we give in to it, we cannot operate smoothly or wisely.

Not only must we face our fears, but we must also get in touch with our faith. We need to find the purpose that Christ can give to our lives that can pull us beyond fear. We have to be in touch with the guiding words and spirit of Jesus that can help us through our fears. We have to see ourselves in the heritage of the disciples who labored despite fear to spread Jesus' word and build his church. The church can be our boat where people need not fear, and we can each help to make it so—for ourselves and for each other.

What are you afraid of? What keeps you from answering the call of Jesus? What keeps you hanging on in your own little boat, clinging for dear life? Are you afraid someone will ask for help and you won't be able to give it? Find people in your church with talents different than your own to help you meet others' needs. Are you afraid you have no talents to offer Jesus? Anyone can come with love and compassion. You don't have to move mountains, just let people know you care. Do what you can and God and others will take care of the rest. Or work with another who balances your talents. Do you fear being laughed at or ridiculed? You might be surprised at how many others have the same fear! We are all in the same boat, and when you realize that, it is half of the battle.

What are you afraid of? Are you sinking in the depths of life, with nothing to hold onto? Do you fear the whole ship is going to sink around you? Get in touch with that fear. Find its roots. Try to understand it and to find ways of dealing with it. What do you fear will happen? What can you do about it? Whom can you talk to about it?

Put yourself in the boat with Jesus and the disciples and remember that he did not criticize the fear. Rather, he combatted the paralyzing effect of it. Fear is not a sin, but doing nothing about it might be. Use your fear to guide you to safety. Don't be afraid to reach out, for help is always there. Ask your pastor. Ask a friend you can trust. No matter what the fear, there is always an answer, and sharing the load makes it lighter too.

Above all, remember that Jesus is in the boat with you. There is always the love and grace of God.

Not nut'n not nobody not no how

Amanda J. Burr

> *Amanda Burr* has a "tentmaking" ministry,
> pastoring First Christian Church of Reseda,
> California, by day and working the night shift as a
> registered nurse in the critical care and emergency
> department of Granada Hills Community Hospital.
> A veteran of the Peace Corps, Amanda holds
> degrees from Columbia University and the School
> of Theology at Claremont. She is the author of
> *New Life for the Old Old Story: A Guide
> for Developing Story Sermons.*

Romans 8:31–39

Our friend the Cowardly Lion of *Wizard of Oz* fame stands outside the door of the great hall where he and his companions await an audience with the wizard. He imagines who and how he will be in the world the moment he is granted his request for courage by the great and powerful Wizard of Oz. Draped in his ermine-collared carpet robe and crowned with a broken flower pot, he sings, "If I were king of the foress, not queen, not duke, not prince," that the rabbits would respect him and the chipmunks would genuflect to him, and so on. When his song is done, his pronouncement is that with courage he wouldn't be afraid of anything: "Not nobody, not no how." His friends ask what about a rhinoceros? "Impossurus." What about a hippopotamus? "I'd trash him from top to bottomus." What about an elephant? "I'd wrap him up in celephant." What about a brontosaurus? "I'd show him who's king of the foress." "How?" they ask. "Courage," he proclaims. What makes a king out of a slave? "Courage." What makes the flag on the mast to wave? "Courage." What makes an elephant charge his tusk? What makes a muskrat guard his musk? "Courage." What makes the Sphinx the Seventh Wonder? "Courage." What makes the dawn come up like thunder? "Courage." What makes the Hottentot so hot?

77

"Courage." What puts the ape in apricot? "Courage." What have they got that I ain't got? "Courage." At this pronouncement before his loving friends, the door to the great hall opens and the four companions plus dog proceed humbly into the presence of the great wizard.

We have all been raised on myths and stories that led us to understand that if we ever met a wizard or a wizardress, we would be in the presence of someone who had mysterious, god-like powers as well as wisdom. In the innocence of childhood, perhaps even our vision of God was something akin to the wizards of the fairy tales we grew up on, someone with long robes and long, snow-white hair and a beard. How like our image of Moses and Merlin was even Michelangelo's depiction of God on the ceiling of the Sistine Chapel. How like the Wizard of Oz is our image of the God who awaits humanity on final judgment day? How many of us in truth have imagined the God of heaven sitting on a throne asking us to give an accounting of our lives, giving on-the-spot answers for the lengthy list of sins that is written on a long roll of paper dangling from God's hand? How many of us have imagined that before we take a single step beyond anything that resembles a pearly gate, we will discuss at length each of these sins and then a verdict will be passed down? In our most intellectually profound moments, we will deny any such notions, but in those most private moments, when we confront what we really don't like about ourselves, or when we add up all that is lacking in ourselves, we may well picture a lengthy *tête-à-tête* with a Wizard of Oz-like God who is waiting to accuse us and call us to account for our misconduct.

Is God the accuser of all humanity? The Wizard of Oz called those who came humbly into his presence names: "So, Tin Man, you say you want a heart? You clinking, clanking, clattering collection of collagenous junk. And you, scarecrow, you come to me for a brain? You billowing bale of bovine fodder." Before the wizard can pronounce the lengthy alliterative descriptive list of the lion's lacks, the lion faints.

I wonder if we, in truth, do not imagine ourselves eventually in the presence of such a one. If we did not imagine God to be such a one, would we ask such questions as "What did I do to deserve this?" and "Why is this happening to me?" Do we not, in fact, picture ourselves standing on the "Last Day" before a tired and disillusioned God who in Wizard of Oz-like fashion might well call each one forward and in a great booming voice say, "So you want to get into heaven, you fidgeting, fussing fossil of

faithless flesh? You simpering, suffering, sullen shell of sophomoric insincerity. Let us first review your sins."

I think we get our ideas about who God is or might be not
from the Bible but from classical literature, movies, myths, and
fairy tales. For if we were to read the Bible, even if we were to
read this passage from Paul's letter to the Romans and were to
believe that what Paul believed was true, we would have the
courage to live in faith. We would not spend hours and hours,
days, weeks, months, even years of our lives as simpering,
suffering, sullen shells of sophomoric insincerity.

If we read and memorized this passage of scripture and
proclaimed it daily in our hearts, we would be hard pressed to
be fidgeting, fussing, fossils of faithless flesh. For as Paul
proclaims to the Romans and for himself, "Not nut'n not nobody
can separate us from the love of God in Christ Jesus, our Lord.
Not nobody, not no how."

Can you hear the triumph in those words? If God is for us,
who is against us? Who is to condemn? It is Christ Jesus who
died, yes, who was raised, who is at the right hand of God, who
indeed intercedes for us. Who will separate us from the love of
Christ? Not hardship, unless we herald it. Not distress, unless
we determine it. Not persecution, unless we propose it. Not
famine, unless we foreordain it. Not nakedness, unless we
intend it. Not peril, unless we premeditate it. Not force, unless
we fathom it. Not nut'n, not nobody, not no how can we separate
ourselves from the love of Jesus Christ unless we ourselves
decline that love. Not death, not life, not angels, not presidents,
emperors, or dictators, not the present time, not the past, not
the future, not powers beyond our control, not distance in height
or depth, time or space, not anything in all creation can
separate you or me from the love that God had for us and still
has for us in Christ Jesus, our Lord.

Not in our affliction, or our disillusionment, not in our
despair, not even when we despise ourselves, can we divest
ourselves of the love of God in Christ Jesus. For Christ Jesus
lived and died for us once and for all time. That event cannot be
erased from human history or from the memory of humanity. If
there were no Bibles for us to read, the love of God in the event
of Jesus would still reach us, carried on the lips of century upon
century of witnesses, and the message would be just as bold and
redeemingly sweet as the printed word in these pages.

Can we courageously enfold ourselves in the notion that
Jesus loved us and continues to love us at our worst and our

best? Can we fathom a love beyond the merely conditional love that we are able to express to one another? Beyond notions of worthiness, proofs of faith and devotion, beyond prerequisite confessions, God loves.

I have heard it said, "God is love." When we know only conditional love, that statement means very little. How much better it is to realize, revelate, and accept that God is actively, consciously, and conscientiously about the business of loving us each and every waking and sleeping moment of this existence. How can we know this? By letting the gift of the life of Jesus be the one real truth in our lives. We can know that loving the Christ of God is loving God. We can know that every day of our lives, the Christ is in touch with God on our behalf, not to make excuses for us or defend us before a great and powerful wizard-like judge, but rather perhaps to put before God our spoken and unspoken prayers, to translate the sighs and groans that echo from the depths of our souls, to celebrate the gleeful laughter, and to call down comfort upon our most confused tears. How can we but love such a one as he? Through Jesus Christ, God is no longer a disapproving parent who only grants love, approval, or favors to the most worthy child. Because the Christ would not be separated from God in hardship, distress, persecutions, famine, nakedness, peril, or death on a cross, because of his immeasurable love, neither can we or will we be cut off from or denied that same active participating love of God.

I do not know if we can manifest or reflect even a fragment of that love in our own lives, but I believe if we will accept it and cherish it, not hoard it or try solely to possess it, that the power of its graciousness may well shine in the best moments of our lives. In my most truthful self, I know that on a good day you will see the Christ in me, and on a bad day I am bound to search for the Christ in me and reconcile myself to the love he offers without conditions. Then and only then will I have the courage to stand and be reconciled to those I have loved only conditionally. Knowing that, through Jesus, not nut'n, not nobody can separate me from God's love, I can venture onward beyond a bad day, humbled and yet encouraged to love again. How, you may ask? "Courage." What makes a human want this life? "Courage." What makes a lover love in spite? "Courage." What makes fear pray through the night? "Courage." What can make the heart lighter than light? "Courage"—and the knowledge that not nut'n, not nobody, not no how can separate us from the love of God! Amen.

$\mathcal{G}$od hears our tears

Janet Hellner-Burris

Janet Hellner-Burris pastors the Christian
Church of Wilkinsburg, Pennsylvania, a small,
dynamic congregation in an inner-city
neighborhood outside of Pittsburgh. She is a
graduate of Princeton Theological Seminary. Janet
became close friends with Mildred, the inspiration
for this sermon, while she was a student at St.
John's College and a VISTA volunteer
in Santa Fe, New Mexico.

Luke 7:11–17

Mildred is a dear, dear friend of mine. I call her my Santa Fe
Mama. She took me into her apartment when I had no place to
live, simply because I was a member of her church and I was a
young person in need. It didn't matter that she was a middle-
aged black woman and I was a young white hippie. She opened
her home and her heart to me. She adopted me and called me
her daughter.

A few weeks ago, I made a quick trip to Santa Fe to see
Mildred and to attend a CPE reunion in Albuquerque. Mildred
had been on my mind a lot these past few months since her
Christmas letter informed me that her only son, Mike, had died
of cancer. I wanted to see her and tell her "I love you" in person.

While we visited that evening, she explained in more detail
Mike's battle with cancer. I felt her pain as tears filled my eyes.
I would have moved heaven and earth to take away that pain,
but I knew that I could not. All I could do for her—and what she
needed most from me—was to sit and listen to her sorrow.

As she poured out her grief and despair, Mildred shared
with me a story she had heard about another woman who had
lost her adult child. This mother talked about the insensitive
and inappropriate remarks well-meaning people make to those

81

who are grieving, especially after the loss of a child—remarks such as:

- "She's better off now," or "At least she isn't suffering anymore"—to which the mother wanted to respond: "Why did she have to suffer at all?"
- "At least you had thirty years together"—to which the mother wanted to reply: "Which year would you choose to have your child die? Children are supposed to die after their parents, not before."
- "I know how you feel"—to which the mother wished she could say: "You can't know how I feel, unless your child has died too."
- "Someday you'll get over it and get on with your life"—to which the mother wanted to say: "I don't think I'll ever get over it. This grief is my life. I live it every day."
- "God doesn't give us more than we can bear"—to which the mother would have answered: "Who decides how much I can bear? God must not know me very well, if God thinks that losing my daughter is bearable."

The story concluded with a piece of advice for those of us who want to know what to say to someone who is grieving: "Please just say how sorry you are. Tell me you won't forget her. Help me share my memories of her. Just let me talk when I need to. And let me cry when I need to."

There are all kinds of griefs we bear: grief over divorce, sickness, disability, unemployment, moving a home, a child leaving home, the end of a friendship—and, of course, the death of a loved one. Yet I have been told, and I am inclined to believe now that I am a mother, that the death of a child is the hardest grief to bear. My visit to Mildred reminded me that even when the child is an adult, the pain is still severe.

What a God-given coincidence that right after my visit with Mildred, my sermon text from the ecumenical lectionary would be about a woman whose son dies.

This passage from Luke reads like a story about bad news on top of bad news on top of bad news. Take a look at verse twelve. It tells us the bad news that someone has died. Luke writes, "A man who had died was being carried out." Now in Jesus' day they did not have coffins, but rather wicker baskets in which they laid their dead. Because the dead were considered unclean, the cemetery was beyond the city's gates. Archaeologists believe that they have found this city and the cemetery, which is about a ten-minute walk from the gate.

So the bad news begins with the announcement of a death. It continues when Luke tells us that the man was young. In those days, as in our own, the death of a young person always was considered a tragedy.

As if this news is not bad enough, Luke then tells us that he was not only a young man but the only son of his mother. For you and for me, this would spell out the tragedy of a parent losing an only child. But in Jesus' day, the death of an only son created a far greater tragedy. This son was to take care of her in her old age. Now he was gone. She had no retirement fund. She had no pension plan, no social security. She had only one son. Now he was dead, and so was her hope for her future security.

Luke casts the final blow when he concludes the bad news with the disclosure that the woman was a widow. This woman had known tragedy before! She had buried her husband, and now she was making that same painful walk to the cemetery to bury her only son. She was all alone! Who would support her in her old age? Who would care for her today? There is a reason why the law of Moses commanded the people to care for the widows and orphans, because they were among the poorest of the poor. For this woman, the death of a husband plus the death of her only son may very well have added up to a life of poverty, hunger, disease, and an early grave.

Obviously, many other people felt this woman's pain, for verse twelve concludes with the information that a large crowd was with her as she made her tearful walk to the cemetery. Attendance at a funeral service was seen in Jewish custom as a work of love—a custom we would do well to continue despite our hectic schedules today.

Then Jesus walks in. Jesus stumbles upon this funeral procession. He sees the widow's tears. He perceives all the different layers of her tragedy, and he is moved deeply. Luke tells us that Jesus responded to her not out of custom, like the crowd, but out of compassion. The Greek word we translate as compassion means, literally, "to be moved to the depths of one's heart." It is a word used only a handful of times in the gospels, because it is a word that describes the deepest kind of emotion we can have for another.

Jesus was not a professional mourner who was paid to cry for the widow and lead the funeral procession. He was not a member of the crowd fulfilling a noble custom. Rather, he was an innocent bystander who allowed himself to be touched to the core of his being.

Now it was not just the human side of Jesus that felt this compassion but his divine side also. My friends, throughout the scriptures we are told over and over again that God feels our pain. Our God is not some unmoved mover who cannot be touched by our sorrow, as the Greek philosopher Aristotle taught. Our God is a God who is intimately involved with us and who even cries with us. Part of the mission of Jesus was to show us this compassionate, feeling side of the God he dared to call "Daddy."

A few years ago, Rev. William Sloan Coffin's twenty-four-year-old son Alex died in an automobile accident. It was a stormy night. Alex lost control of the car and it sank into the Boston Harbor. The next Sunday Rev. Coffin preached a sermon in which he described his grief and God's:

> The one thing that should never be said when someone dies is, "It is the will of God." Never do we know enough to say that. My consolation lies in knowing that it was not the will of God that Alex died; that when the waves closed over the sinking car, God's was the first of all our hearts to break.

This image of God's heart being the first to break is the best description I have heard of God's compassion for us. It is the best answer I have heard to the question of where is our loving God in the midst of tragedy.

I remembered Dr. Coffin's sermon that night in Santa Fe when Mildred asked me the question that has haunted believers since the beginning of human existence: "Why? Why does a loving God allow such suffering? Where is God when we need God the most?" Through my tears I told her that I had no real answers for her, nothing that would take away her pain. "All I can tell you, Mildred, is that God's heart was breaking too when you stood by Mike's hospital bed and watched him slowly wither away. God was in that room with you and Mike. God was suffering with Mike. God was crying with you. God felt your pain, because Mike was God's precious child too."

Now some of you may ask, "But if God is all powerful, why didn't God cure Mike of the cancer? After all, enough people were praying for him." I don't know. As a person who lives by faith, I find that I have to live with a lot of questions. I don't have all the answers to why bad things happen to good people. But

I do know about God's power to resurrect. In the story from Luke, Jesus uses this power to raise the widow's son from death. Yet the power of God's resurrection is far greater than the power of God to give our loved ones life after death. The power of God's resurrection spills over into this life so that we who are the survivors of these tragedies can live with our sorrow and can overcome the deadly despair. The power of God's resurrection is the power God gives to us slowly, but surely, to pick up the pieces, wrap up our wounds, and create a new life for ourselves.

This power of the resurrection to create new life on both sides of the grave is what Paul described to the Romans when he said, "We know that all things work together for good for those who love God, who are called according to his purpose" (Romans 8:28).

Of course, Mildred cannot see any good coming out of Mike's death now. It would be cruel and insensitive to quote this verse to her as though it would take away her pain. It took me five years to see what God has been doing in my life after my brother's death to cancer. All I can say to her is that the power of the resurrection kept me alive when, at first, I didn't want to be. Then slowly, over the course of several years, this resurrecting power raised me from my despair to a new life with new joys and new loved ones to care about.

I will be mailing this sermon tape to Mildred, and I can just hear her say at this point, "But I'm too old for a new life"—to which I would respond with a smile and many tears, "You're still young to me, dear friend, and I would guess that God isn't finished with you yet, even though you want God to be. What God doesn't complete on this side of your grave, God will finish on the other side when God sends Mike to take you home to be with the Lord. Meanwhile, I'm here for you. I'm not afraid to listen to you and walk with you in your pain. And I believe, with all my heart, that God is here too. God hears our tears. God's heart is breaking too. Our loving, compassionate, tender God will see us through these days of pain."

O Lord, we pray for all who feel the pain of bereavement today, especially the widows and those who have lost their children. Help us to be sensitive to their feelings of anger, despair, and doubt. Help us to listen and to gently help them to build a new life for themselves. Stay close by their side, Lord, even when they reject you. May they come to see your compassion and your power to raise them from the pits of despair to new life. In the name of our Lord Jesus Christ, the Healer, we pray. Amen.

*C*an you stand the rain?

Cynthia L. Hale

Cynthia Hale is founding pastor of the Ray of Hope Christian Church in Decatur, Georgia. A former federal prison chaplain, she has degrees from Hollins College, Duke University, and United Theological Seminary. Cynthia is currently president of the minister's fellowship of the National Convocation of the Christian Church.

Matthew 7:24–27

For the past several weeks, Georgia has been inundated with rain. Heavy rains, disturbing rains, life-threatening rains. Rains that flood your backyard and fill your life with gloom. We are fair-weather folks. We like sunny days and blue skies. We can deal with the sun shining. But the question is, "Can we stand the rain?"

Seasons change, as you well know, and the weather is unpredictable: Flash storms come without warning, blue skies quickly turn to gray. What appeared to be a perfect day abruptly comes to an end. You were handling the sun. The question is, "Can you stand the rain?"

Life is unpredictable. One minute you're up, the next you're down. One minute everything is under control, the next all hell breaks loose. In a second, all that you've worked for, studied for, prayed, saved, and waited patiently for is suddenly wiped out. You were enjoying the showers of blessing. Now the question is, "Can you stand the rain?"

Jesus is concluding a series of teaching on the Kingdom and requirements for its citizens in his well-known Sermon on the Mount. In this collection of teachings, Jesus carefully lays out the standards for godly and victorious living as a Christian in the world.

86

The words that Jesus spoke to his disciples and the multitudes who stopped to listen as he sat among them on the mountainside were straight-from-the-heart counsel of God. Jesus had no problem sharing with folks the fact that the words that he spoke were not his, but the Father's who sent him.

The words that Jesus spoke were words of wisdom and instruction in righteousness for those who desired to live according to God's will and with God's blessing.

If persons wanted to master the art of living and ensure that they could deal with life with all of its blessings and curses, all of its uncertainties, all he or she had to do was take heed to the words of Jesus. The words of Jesus represented the wisdom of the author of life, and who can better instruct one in the mastery of anything than its creator?

Jesus says as much in his concluding remarks in his Sermon on the Mount when he states, "Everyone then who hears these words of mine and acts on them will be like a wise man who built his house on rock. The rain fell, the floods came, and the winds blew and beat on that house, but it did not fall, because it had been founded on rock" (Matthew 7:24–25).

Notice how practical Jesus is in his illustration and application. To make his point about the stability of a person's life, their character, he uses an illustration that his hearers could easily identify with. Jesus tells the story of two builders, contrasting their methods of building to illustrate the importance of how one builds and the possible results or outcome of one's building.

There is a wise builder and a foolish one. Both are building a house. The wise builder is the one who builds his or her house on the rock. The foolish one builds on the sand. Now everyone should know that it is better to build one's house on the rock because rock provides a more solid foundation than sand.

But in Jesus' days there were careless, lazy persons, as unfortunately is the case today, who were looking for the easiest way to do things. Throughout Palestine, there were riverbeds that dried up in the summer, leaving a smooth and inviting sandy place called a *wadi*. Persons looking for a place to build their houses were attracted to these *wadis*. They looked stable enough.

A wise person would investigate to determine whether or not there was rock under the sandy surface. But the foolish person wasn't interested in going deeper. He or she was only willing to do what was necessary and not willing to put in any extra effort.

As long as it was summer, everything was just fine; as long as the sun was shining, everything was safe. But then the seasons changed—summer turned to fall and fall to winter. Winter in Palestine is the rainy season. When the rain came, those dried riverbeds were quickly filled with raging water that beat against those houses along with the wind and tested the stability and durability of them.

The wise person's house built on the rock stood firm, the foolish person's house built on the sand fell with a great crash.

Such is life, Jesus was saying. A person's life and character is like a house: It must be built carefully, not carelessly. How one builds, the materials one chooses, will determine the quality and durability of it.

Every house will be tested. Contrary to our desires, the sun won't shine forever. Providence has different seasons. Into each life some rain must fall. No one can escape it.

When I talk about rain, I'm not talking about the gentle showers that cool us off, calm us, and refresh us. I'm talking about storms that test us, try us, and prove us. Some of these storms are heavier than others.

Rain in our life represents rough places in our journey, such as sickness or sorrow. Rain can be the death of a relative or a relationship. Rain can be equated to an unhappy home where love is absent and mutual respect and responsibility is not recognized. Rain is the pain of living alone or the absence of a significant other in your life. Rain is the hurt you feel when you've been walked on, talked about, lied to, or mistreated by someone you thought was your friend.

Rain is the gnawing temptations that are ever present with their attractive offers leading you either to despair or destruction. Rain is simply being black in America, or a woman, and having always to be better than the best even on your worst day or when you're just not feeling up to it.

Rain is also the awareness that you did not make it or you may not make it to wherever you're heading and having to decide what that says about who you are and your sense of worth.

Rain is discovering that you did not make the grades you should have; your telephone, television, and dating privileges are gone for a month and those same friends you used to talk about others with will now be talking about you.

Rain is coming home to find that your place has been broken into, your child or a loved one is on drugs, you've been laid off or fired, your finances are depleted, your utilities are about to be or have been turned off.

Into every life some rain will fall! Can you stand the rain? It all depends on how you build your house. Only a house built on a firm foundation can withstand the rain. Only a life whose foundations are sure can stand the test. It all depends on how you build your life, the kind of foundation and material you use.

Jesus said, "Everyone then who hears these words of mine and acts on them will be like a wise man who built his house on rock." The wise person builds her house to withstand anything.

In building your life, the only firm foundation you can build on is Christ and his words. Everything else is sinking sand. All the world's philosophies and all the world's wisdom pale in the face of the light of God's word of truth. They are like grass.

Isaiah says, "The grass withers, the flower fades; but the word of our God will stand forever" (Isaiah 40:8). The word of the Lord is eternal. It stands firm in the heavens. You can depend on it, you can build on it, you can stand anything when you're in it and it is in you.

The word of God is living; it is life. All spiritual life comes from it. The word of God through faith will work in us the very thing that it commands or promises. Nothing can resist its power when received into the heart through the Holy Spirit.

The word builds character. It is like a seed; when planted in our hearts, it will sprout and grow slowly, hidden and unobserved. It is the power of God at work, developing, building in us all that we need for life and living.

The word has power to lighten our darkness. In our hearts, it will bring the light of God, the assurance of God's love, the knowledge of God's will, the fullness of God's grace. The word will fill us with strength and courage to conquer every enemy and to do whatever God asks us to do. The word can cleanse, sanctify, develop faith and obedience, and become in us the seed of every character trait of our Lord.

It is the wise man or woman, boy or girl, who builds his or her life by hearing the word of God *and* putting it into practice.

Listening to the word of God isn't difficult for most of us. It is our joy, particularly, as black folks. We love good preaching. We will travel from church to church, meeting to meeting, looking for a good preacher.

Our mind's delight is in having the truth clearly presented. Our imaginations are gratified by its illustration, our emotions are stirred by its application. To the active mind, knowledge gives pleasure, but we have mistaken the pleasure we have in hearing for spirituality and worship.

We are content to listen like the folks God talked about to the prophet Ezekiel: "They come to you as people come, and they sit before you as my people, and they hear your words, but they will not obey them....To them you are like a singer of love songs, one who has a beautiful voice and plays well on an instrument; they hear what you say, but they will not do it" (Ezekiel 33:31–32).

Listening to the words of God is only the beginning. Jesus said, "Everyone who hears these words of mine and puts them into practice is like a wise person...."

We must listen to God's word with the objective of applying it to our lives and living it. The word has no power in one's life unless it is obeyed. It must be applied.

It's like receiving medication from a doctor: The medication has no effect until you take it. The word of God must be taken, applied to one's life, and lived.

When you study and are obedient to God's word daily, you are building a strong life and character. Obedience to Christ and his word is the only sure foundation. Life founded on Christ the rock can stand any test.

Can you stand the rain?

If you're living a life that is built on surface values, surface commitments, attending church out of habit or for entertainment, listening to the word for inspiration only and not obeying, you're standing on shaky ground.

But if your life is firmly rooted and grounded in Christ and his word, let the storms rise, let the rain come, let the winds blow, let the streams rise.

> Our hope is built on nothing less
> Than Jesus' blood and righteousness
> I dare not trust the sweetest frame
> But wholly lean on Jesus' name.
>
> His oath, his covenant, his blood
> Support me in the whelming flood.
> When all around my world give way
> He then is all my hope and stay.
>
> On Christ the solid rock I stand.
> All other ground is sinking sand.
> All other ground is sinking sand.

$\mathcal{F}$ools for Christ

Kelly Boyte Peters

Kelly Boyte Peters is the associate minister of
Lakewood Congregational Church (United Church
of Christ) in suburban Cleveland, Ohio, and an
ordained Disciple. A graduate of Kalamazoo College
and Vanderbilt Divinity School, she is the coauthor
of *Spiritual Growth in the Congregation* and has
written for *The Disciple*, the *United Church
News*, and other publications.

1 Corinthians 1:18–25

My most memorable April Fool's Day caper occurred when
I was about fourteen years old. That year, April Fool's Day fell
on a Saturday. I was out baby-sitting on Friday night and got
home about 11:30. I waved good-bye to the folks who drove me
home, went into my house, got my pajamas and slippers on, and
then left the house and crossed the street to where my friend
Colleen lived. As was the plan, I woke her up by knocking lightly
on her bedroom window. She woke up and opened the window.
Then I crawled in and she crawled out. I spent the night in her
house and she in mine. The next morning when my mother
stuck her head in my bedroom door, Colleen's dark curly hair
startled her and Colleen delightedly shouted, "April Fools!"
When Colleen's father, looking sleepy and very much in need of
a cup of coffee, woke up *me* instead of his daughter, it took him
a few minutes to realize that it was funny. We were so proud of
ourselves for concocting such a scheme—so much more sophis-
ticated, we thought, than junior-high pranks like loosening the
top of the salt shaker.

Today is April Fool's Day and a Sunday and I couldn't resist
having us reflect on the apostle Paul's words about wisdom and
foolishness. In this sermon to the Corinthian church, Paul is

91

exhorting the people to greater faithfulness to the gospel by distinguishing the wisdom of the world from God's wisdom. Paul wants to strengthen this beloved congregation by helping them understand that in their new identity as Christians, they are called to see the world in new ways. They will no longer be able to be citizens both of the world and of God's community. As Christians, they see the world with new eyes. They see that many of the values of the world clash with the values of God. As Paul puts it, what looks like wisdom in the world is foolishness to God. And what looks like foolishness in the world is wisdom to God.

Paul's words contain a warning. "You're going to be laughed at for your faith. You'll be ridiculed and labeled a fool because of your belief in the story of God's love made flesh." Paul wants to prepare the people for future difficulties. It's almost as if he's saying, "Claim your identity now, before you have to defend yourself. Go ahead and call yourselves 'Fools for Christ!'" (See 1 Corinthians 4:10.)

What does Paul mean when he uses the word *fool*?

He does *not* mean that Christians are to be unthinking, that we're not to use our heads. Elsewhere in the gospel, we're told to be shrewd and wise. We know of Jesus' own teaching and studying and his regard for the intellectual tradition of the rabbi. So Paul is not calling for an abandonment of the brain in the faith journey.

Rather, a fool is defined as someone whose actions are determined solely by love. A fool for Christ does not live by the values of the world. Her actions are not determined by profit. His motives are not tied to revenge. Their lives are not lived even according to the traditional views of what's right and wrong. A fool is someone whose actions are determined solely by asking the question, "What is the loving thing to do?"

The gospels are full of examples of such foolish behavior. I have selected three examples for us to look at—all from the parables. These parables describe for us what life is like when lived in God's realm and under God's rule—an experience we look forward to in the future but which we glimpse now, from time to time.

In each of these parables, listen for the voice of foolishness—acts of foolishness of love.

Scene #1: A shepherd is closing the day. He's hot and tired and is putting all the sheep into the fold for the night. As each one enters the corral, he counts—96, 97, 98, 99.... He counts again. Sure enough, he's missing one sheep. One animal is out in the pasture, lost and possibly in danger. If he leaves the flock, the shepherd might lose more sheep because the gate is not secure without him.

The wisdom of the world says, "Don't do it—it's too risky! Don't even think about the life of one when you should be concerned for the many." But God's wisdom says, "I will not let one of my creatures be lost. I will leave the 99 to find the one who is lost and I will bring it back to the fold." So the shepherd, in a move that would have been ridiculed by other shepherds, did just that.

Scene #2: A man is walking down a road and sees a man on the other side of the road in desperate need. He's wounded and looks as if he's been beaten. "It would do no good just to give him some money," the man thinks. "If I go over there, I'll have to get involved."

The wisdom of the world shouts clearly at this point, "No! It's too dangerous! You never know—maybe it's a hoax. And besides, you're a Samaritan. Would anyone stop and help you? Do you really want to spend your whole day with this guy? Let someone else do it." But God's wisdom shouts back just as clearly, "Act in love. Whenever you feed the hungry or clothe the naked, you're expressing love to me." And so the Samaritan played the part of God's loving fool, carrying the man to an inn, bandaging his wounds, and leaving him with sufficient money and provisions.

Scene #3: An old, lonely man is taking a walk around his property. He can't feel much pride in his accomplishments, can't take pride in his farm or in the loyalty of his servants or in the diligence of his elder son, because he's simply overwhelmed with sadness at the loss of his younger son who left home months ago. "Is he safe?" "What is he doing?" and "Will he ever come home?" are the questions the father asks himself daily. As he peers down the road, his thoughts heavy on his mind, he can almost see his son's figure walking toward him. The old man looks down, certain his imagination has run wild, then he glances back up. Yes, it's true. The boy gets closer, runs to his father, and breathlessly begins to spurt out the speech he'd practiced. "Father, I've squandered my inheritance. I'm no longer worthy to be called your son. Just let me work for you and eat the food of the animals."

At this point in the scene, the wisdom of the world would say, "Teach him a lesson. Let him see the consequences of his actions. Let him work for you for a while and think about his behavior." But God's wisdom asks, "What is the loving thing to do?" and this wise father speaks the foolishly loving words, "My son, you were dead and are now alive now. Welcome home and let's celebrate."

These three scenes show us what life is like in the realm of God, where there is no interest in revenge but great interest in forgiveness. In the realm of God, risks are taken on behalf of individuals. In the realm of God, actions that are safe are spurned for actions that are loving. When the wisdom of the world said, "Don't heal on the Sabbath," Jesus said the law of love is greater and he healed anyway. In the realm of God, love is the sole determining factor. In the realm of God, only fools can be citizens.

For those of you who are joining Lakewood Congregational Church today, I have a special message just for you: Joining the church is one of the most foolish decisions you can make. Let me tell you what you can expect after you join.

We're going to ask you to give away your money. The wisdom of the world will tell you to save and to invest, but we'll ask you to give it away.

We're going to ask you to give up your time. The wisdom of the world will tell you to make time for yourself, to take up time-saving procedures in the office and the kitchen, and to lobby for more leisure time. But we're going to ask you to give up your leisure time for projects such as Habitat for Humanity or cooking a meal for the community dinner or baby-sitting in our nursery or even, heaven forbid, serving on a committee.

Furthermore, we'll ask you to get up early on Sunday mornings. And I can't promise you you'll like everything you'll hear after you get here.

Yes, joining this church is one of the most foolish things you can do. But be comforted by the thought that God loves fools. And if someone asks you tomorrow if you were a part of any April Fool's Day prank, you can smile and tell them that you were a part of the greatest foolishness of all.

Welcome, new members, to this group of God's people, trying our best to be foolish enough to feel at home in God's realm.

$\mathcal{T}$he art of making bread

Beverly Dale

Beverly Dale is executive director of a century-old campus ministry called the Christian Association at the University of Pennsylvania. Born and raised in Illinois, Beverly is a graduate of Chicago Theological Seminary and preached this sermon at Colfax, Illinois, where she served as pastor.

Jeremiah 31:31–34 and John 6:33–34

The first time I baked bread, I was told to knead it a long time. This meant pushing the dough and folding the dough over and over to allow plenty of air to get into it. The more air that is kneaded into the bread, the lighter it becomes. I was instructed in this age-old art by several 4-H leaders, my aunt, who was the family specialist in bread making, and my mother, who saw it as her maternal responsibility to raise a daughter who was an outstanding cook. As a result of the hours of their instruction and the hours spent practicing, I eventually became very good at making yeast breads. And I didn't even need to follow the recipe.

One older person writes of the spiritual journey by saying, "My sin is my dismay at studying the recipe for all those years, and never baking the bread." I had spent hours and hours kneading bread dough, shaping the dough into rolls, waiting by the oven for the golden color, and inhaling that exquisite aroma of fresh baked bread still hot in the pan. How sad that someone would spend the same amount of time just studying, just preparing, just wondering if they could or should bake the bread. What a shame to stand aside and ask, "Do I have the right ingredients? The best quality? Do I have the skills? Do I have the time and the energy to invest? Do I have the correct instructions?"

The old way of following God through obedience to the law was like "following the recipe." However, in Jeremiah 31:31–34, we read that God was going to establish a new covenant that would be written on human hearts. Even though we claim to be under this new covenant, there are many of us who still spend our time studying and following the recipe. In so doing, we may never get on with the creative process of life in the Spirit— actually "baking the bread."

In our Christian lives, if the recipe is our focus, we will spend our lives concerned about obeying God with exact prescriptions: "This is exactly how everyone is to live if they are really Christians." "These are the rules for a Christian life—the requirements and expectations." "This is how we know who is one of us." The "recipe" of obedience to the "letter of the law" becomes a litmus test, a prejudgment as to the expected result.

To focus only on the recipe creates dilemmas, such as one recipe calling for one-fourth cup of margarine while another calls for three tablespoons of butter and the end product is supposed to be the same. Which is correct? What is the difference between margarine and butter? There is a small measurable difference between one-fourth cup and three tablespoons as well: How will that difference affect the outcome?

When the focus remains on the recipe, the baker becomes overly concerned and even stymied about the "letter" of the instructions. Baking never becomes a creative process but remains a legalistic exercise. The new covenant spoken of in Jeremiah means we are to focus on the baking process and on the finished product. And the best way to do that is to put the recipe in our hearts.

We all know that this is what makes the best bakers. These creative cooks know that variations in the recipe probably won't destroy the product but may even enhance it. They take the risk of following the heart and are then free to dive into the joy of creating the finished product: a pleasing aroma, a delightful taste.

When I was baking bread, my brothers and sisters would eventually follow their noses into the kitchen. They would gather around the kitchen table, enjoying the smells and savoring the taste of fresh baked bread. As Christians, we are invited to partake of the bread of life that gives life to the world. When the law of God is written on our hearts and we walk in the Spirit, it is our very lives that offer up a pleasing aroma to God.

In short, to eat the bread of life is to partake in Jesus' life— to walk in Jesus' footprints, to live in loving and compassionate ways, to heal wounded lives and oppose injustice. It is to surrender the safety of a recipe and follow the leading of the Spirit moving within our hearts. It is to give up thinking we run our lives best by obedience to a set prescription, a moral code. Instead, it is to rely on the Spirit's whispered instructions in our ears.

It is scary to give up the rules, the "shoulds" and "oughts" that someone else simply handed down. It is scary to take the risk because we may fail. How many of us cooks have thought, "I know this recipe by heart," but when it is tried, we had forgotten some key ingredient? The result? We really botch it! When this happens in our walk of faith, God's response is to say, "It's OK." That is grace.

When I made my very first pie, my family made a big to-do about the event—probably because they knew that in an hour or so, they could eat the benefits of my experimenting. I followed the instructions the best that I could. We even took a picture of it before putting it into the oven. Sure enough, it looked as if my first pie was going to be a big success. I had followed the recipe down to the letter. When it was time to take it out of the oven, I grabbed two pot holders and reached in—only to drop my prize upside down!

I was crushed. The "pie" was all over the oven. My family, however, grabbed spoons and spatulas and piled it back into the pan and filled the plates. They quickly gobbled it down and pronounced it the best pie they had ever eaten. That was grace! I knew it was the sorriest pie you could ever lay eyes on. I knew there was nothing great about that mess. But the message to me was plain: "So you botched it this time. It's OK." And that is God's message to us, over and over again.

God is not concerned that the bread of our lives be top-notch, blue-ribbon quality. We are not called to become saints. Instead, God calls us to commit the recipe to heart, to fire up the ovens and get on with our purpose: lovingly to care for one another, to be watchful for injustice, to show compassion—and to be grace-filled toward one another when we fail ourselves and others and botch it up...as we surely will do.

I quit baking bread years ago. I no longer remember any recipes. I'm sure I've forgotten all the tips and hints and careful instructions I was taught. My bread-making activities are but a memory now.

Neither can we as Christians assume that, because years ago we once said "yes" to God, we can now pull off a Christian lifestyle with little effort. Partaking of the bread of life is an ongoing process, of listening, of reflecting—of seeking to discern what God requires of me and then daring to do it.

Is the recipe written on our hearts? Let's fire up the ovens. God awaits our pleasing aroma.

$\mathcal{W}$e know the words— we need lives to match!

Mary Louise Rowand

Mary Louise Rowand, of Dallas, Texas, doesn't
know the meaning of the word *retire*. Currently a
member of the boards of trustees of Texas Christian
University, Brite Divinity School, and the
American Bible Society, Mary Louise is in wide
demand as a speaker both at home and abroad.
She is past president of ICWF and Church
Women United, and with her husband E. C.
has traveled in over 190 countries.

Matthew 13:3a and Luke 15:3–32

How do you preach in a world that's changing?
When everything you say needs rearranging,
Where truth is no longer the simple truth,
And not even proof is absolute proof!

God? Once we knew Him, but we outgrew Him!
Now we only misconstrue Him when we try
To do our God-explaining,
For the words that are remaining
Call up images we have to qualify!

> *"Sure As You're Born"*
> *Musical Revue by Kramer and Bentser*

Our national spiritual hunger is overwhelming, from the most illiterate and lowly to those who walk around with more money than God, in houses where no love is!

Our whole country seems to be embarked on a spiritual quest. It's a national phenomenon: theologians and historians trying to give an accounting of the "world we have" and "why we have lost it."

99

It is the same old question. Every generation asks it. *What is the single most important need in the American church today? More members? More money? More programs?*

If I were to answer, I would say that what we need most is *a rediscovery of the mind, message, and mission of Jesus as found in the four Gospels.* I know they are very old words, but we seem to have forgotten them for a very long time! *This* is the need of every new generation of Christians!

It is very easy in our eagerness to serve him through our complicated organizational structures, through what we call the business of the church, in our conventions and assemblies and proclamations and creeds...and very easy to forget the *primary* reason for our existence.

Dostoevski, that most outstanding of all modern Russian writers, in his finest novel *The Brothers Karamazov*, recognized this condition in the church of his day. In the chapter "The Grand Inquisitor," he expresses his feelings in a chilling and terrifying story. The setting: the days of the Spanish Inquisition, in Seville. Jesus has just returned to earth. He has come to Seville and is walking toward the massive Gothic cathedral in the vast square. A funeral procession is also slowly moving toward the cathedral steps. The only child of a widow has died. Her little casket is being carried to the cathedral. Suddenly, the people see Jesus and they recognize him immediately. He has come back as he promised. Here he is among them now, the one to whom all their prayers and hopes have been directed. He can give new life to this innocent little girl as he did long ago in Palestine.

The people call to him, and he goes to them. They cry out, "Heal this child!" The mother falls on her knees in front of him. "Have mercy on me. If you will, you can put new life into my child." He pauses, then raising both hands high into the air, he cries out to his God, "Let this child live!" And to the utter amazement of everyone, the child moves, sits up surrounded by all the flowers, smiles, and calls out to her mother. The people begin to chant, "He has come to us! He has come! He has come!:

However, standing in the shadows of the cathedral is the Grand Inquisitor, the powerful cardinal of the church. What he has seen he does not like. He sees Jesus' arrival not as an occasion for rejoicing, but as a threat to his authority. So the cardinal has Jesus arrested and placed in a solitary prison cell. Late that night, the cardinal comes alone to visit his royal prisoner.

"Why have you come?" he demands. "We no longer have need of you! We are now in charge of your church. We know how to run it well. Why have you come back to disturb our peace and authority? Leave us now. Do not come back. We have no need of you!" Dostoevski has Jesus look long and lovingly into the empty eyes of the cardinal...and then, Jesus stands, walks across the cell, and kisses the cardinal lightly on his thin, bloodless lips. Then Jesus walks out of the cell, leaving the cardinal alone with his great cathedral.

I agree, this is an extreme example of the church forgetting its master. Yet, like all hyperbole, there are times when we need a spiritual shock treatment to bring us face-to-face with a great truth.

I am convinced that if the church of our time is not as attractive and compelling as it ought to be, perhaps the problem may be that we have cut ourselves off from the taproot of our faith! We need to rediscover the source!

Why do we come here to worship, Sunday after Sunday, fifty-two Sundays a year, for five, ten, thirty years—or a whole lifetime? Getting up early Sunday morning, getting ready, getting the children dressed, driving over in all sorts of weather, sometimes not feeling too well ourselves, angry at the government, worried about our health and financial problems, dressed in our best and on our best behavior, walking into the building, greeting friends, singing hymns, praying prayers, reading scripture, listening to sermons, bringing our offering, taking the bread and cup....We call it the worship of God, *but why do we do this?*

I'm sure there are many reasons, but deep down inside I feel we do this in the hope that we might get to know Jesus of Nazareth better. We are seeking our primary source! And to know him better, perhaps our lives will be better, perhaps the world a better place. In reality, are we not here seeking Jesus?

If the world around us seems to be falling apart—if in government, education, the political arena, sports, morals, ethics, and business, we are confronted with a terrible sadness that our heroes have clay feet—then who can we trust? To whom can we go for assurance? Who will tell us the truth? Who will welcome us, accept us as we are, love us, forgive us, and plant fresh hope in our lives? Is this not the promise of the Nazarene? He is the one who dared to say: "I am the way, the truth, and the life. I am the bread of life. I am the Good Shepherd. I am the light of the world!"

Recently, Pope John Paul said, "A divided Church is a poor message to a broken, divided world!" For the past twenty years, we have been losing thousands of church members a year! So we come here as seekers demanding that our worship be honest in its search for the source!

Annie Dillard, one of my favorite contemporary writers, says, "I know only enough of God that I want to worship him, by any means ready at hand." She tells of worship in a simple white frame church in the forest close to her home: "On a good Sunday, perhaps twenty are there. I am the only person under sixty. The members are a mixed denomination; the minister is a Congregationalist, and wears a white shirt. The man knows God! Once in the middle of the long pastoral prayer of intercession for the whole world, the gift of wisdom for its leaders, for hope and mercy for the grieving and pained, succor to the oppressed, and God's grace to all—in the middle of this he stopped, and burst out, 'Lord , we bring you the *same* petitions every week!'—after a shocked pause, he continued reading his prayer. Because of this, I like him very much."[1]

To rediscover the essence of Jesus, we must go back to his parables. As we grapple with them, we soon discover what *he* felt were his most vital truths. One day he said, "The kingdom of heaven is like a merchant in search of fine pearls; on finding one pearl of great value, he went and sold all that he had and bought it" (Matthew 13:45–46).

And what is Jesus saying here? I believe that he is saying *all* of us must make for ourselves a primary decision about our relationship with God! Our lives are filled with all sorts of pearls: the "pearls" of our comfortable home, our delicacies food, our cherished friendships, our educational achievements, our families, our health, our American freedom—wonderful things, all of them, *and* they are all to be cherished, and nurtured, and profoundly appreciated. *Yet, they must not be our God!*

C.S. Lewis, that Cambridge University intellectual, had forsaken his early Christian beliefs for a sophisticate atheism. One day while reading of the faith of another Englishman (George MacDonald, in *Phantastes*), he was profoundly moved spiritually. He had not found the "pearl of great price," *but* God had found *him*, and placed it in his hands. Lewis said, "It was as though the voice which had called to me from the world's end was now speaking at my side!"

Our contemporary world is full of this same sort of confrontation. People on drugs make anguished decisions to stop. People who have lived selfishly see themselves for what they have become and make the decision to change. Others whose lives have become narrow and bitter become compassionate and forgiving. The man whose "god" has become his job, or his materialistic possessions, or his driving ambition, one day realizes that no matter how complete life seems to be, it is never complete without God at the center!

And finally, we realize that it is true: "Our hearts are restless until they find their rest in Thee" (St. Augustine). That's what Jesus was saying in his parable of the pearl of great price. We must make a decision about God!

And what is this God like? Tell us, Jesus, why is God the pearl of great price? Convince us, Jesus, that this God is worthy of our allegiance! Tell us about your God! Is God in charge? Tell us what God is really like! As one of the disciples, Philip, said one day, "Lord, show us the Father, and we shall be satisfied!" That's our question too. In a world where evil too often seems to win, where bad things happen to good people, what is God like?

He gave them this answer: He ran three parables together, all linked up to a common theme. He was trying to tell that the primary, basic, fundamental nature of his God is *love*, and *caring*, and never-endingly *seeking us out with grace and forgiveness!*

The disciples had been brought up on the notion that God was primarily a terrible, angry judge, who did good things for good people, and vented bad things on bad people! God was not something to be loved, but feared!

Into this mass of bad information, Jesus dared to toss three spiritual hand grenades, which blew away this theology of fear. He said, "Which one of you, having a hundred sheep and losing one of them, does not leave the ninety-nine in the wilderness and go after the one that is lost until he finds it? When he has found it, he lays it on his shoulders and rejoices" (Luke 15:4–5). That's what God is really like! No matter *who* you are, or *where* you are, the loving, compassionate God never gives up on you!

Then Jesus said to them, "What woman having ten silver coins, if she loses one of them, does not light a lamp, sweep the house" (Luke 15:8)—and look under every rug and every piece of furniture, sweeping, cleaning, searching...until she finds it?

How happy she is! In her rejoicing, she runs to all her neighbors crying out, "Come to my house. Rejoice with me. I've made fresh tea and special cookies. Let's have a party. I have found the coin I had lost! That's what God is really like! If you care that much about a coin, just imagine how much more God cares about you!"

Then, before they could digest his stories about a lost sheep and a lost coin, Jesus told them of a lost boy. Yes, yes, we all know this story so well. At one time or another, all of us have been like that lost boy in a far country.

But the story is *not* really about the lost boy who finally does come home. The focus of the parable is on the *waiting, loving, compassionate, forgiving father!* We call it the parable of the prodigal son, but it is really the parable of the forgiving father!

The turning point of the story is not when the lost boy decides to come home, *but* while the boy was far, far off down the road, the father, who has been sitting at his window day after day for months, sees his son off in a great distance—recognizes his form, his shape, his special walk—and the father has compassion, and he starts running as fast as his old legs will take him, and he takes his son in his arms, holds him tight, kisses him, and speaks words of love and forgiveness!

Back at the house, the father gives his son the best robe he has, so as to cover up his old rags. He puts a ring of renewed household authority on his finger. He fits him out with the finest shoes in the house. He brings forth the fatted calf for a great feast, and the father says, "Let us eat and celebrate; for this son of mine was dead and is alive again; he was lost and is found!" (Luke 15:23–24). *That* is what God is like, said Jesus. No wonder our commitment to *that* God is like finding the pearl of great price.

I began by asking, "How do you preach in a world that's changing?" We need to go back to his parables to rediscover what Jesus holds out as good news for our day!

I am convinced that the parables of Jesus are *not* merely prescriptions for better individuals, but also they are prescriptions for a better society. If we are living in a time with a sense of betrayal, where many people are bogged down in pessimism, then what do the parables have to say to our social order?

On a recent trip to England, I stood on Dover Beach, just under the famous White Cliffs. The sun was bright on that winter day, but the strong wind blowing in off the water was like sharp fingers of ice cutting through our heavy coats. I thought of Matthew Arnold's poem, "Dover Beach," as he gave his assessment of his time:

...The world, which *seems*
To lie before us like a land of dreams,
So various, so beautiful, so new,

Hath really neither joy, nor love, nor light,
Nor certitude, nor peace, nor help for pain;
And we are here as on a darkling plain
Swept with confused alarms of struggle and flight,
Where ignorant armies clash by night.

Up against that pessimistic view of the world, place the person and the teaching of Jesus of Nazareth. Hear and remember his words: "I have said these things to you so that my joy may be in you, and that your joy may be complete" (John 15:11). "I am the light of the world" (John 8:12). "This is my commandment, that you love one another as I have loved you" (John 15:12). "In the world you face persecution. But take courage; I have conquered the world!" (John 16:33).

So, there *is* joy, and love, and light, and certitude, and peace, and help for pain, Mr. Arnold!

This is the good news of the church. This is the essence of our worship celebration! And this is why our individual faith can make a difference in our social structures.

We know the *words*! We need lives to *match*!

---

[1]Annie Dillard, *Holy the Firm*. Harper & Row, 1988, pp. 55, 57f.

*H*aunted

Rebecca Z. Brown

Rebecca Brown is co-pastor of First Christian
Church in Findlay, Ohio, with her husband David.
She is a graduate of Phillips University, magna
cum laude, and Lexington Theological Seminary.
The Browns served on the theological school faculty
in Bolenge, Zaire, under the auspices of the
Division of Overseas Ministries. Rebecca preached
this sermon for itineration purposes upon
returning from Africa.

Mark 12:38–44

When I was just a little girl, my family moved into our brand new home. It was complete with a great big unfinished basement—a great big unfinished haunted basement, to be exact. Lurking in the shadows of the furnace and water heater or occasionally lying wait under the stairs was none other than *Skeleton Man!* The sole goal and only purpose of the bag of bones' existence was to kidnap me. What he was going to do with me I had no idea, but he was there waiting for me to go into the basement alone...so of course I never did, despite the fact that some of my favorite toys were there.

I don't really remember how long Skeleton Man haunted me, but in my life he was very real and his existence troubled me. I told my family about him and no matter how hard I tried to forget him, or ignore him, I couldn't. He haunted me.

It's been a long time now since I've been haunted by something along the lines of Skeleton Man. I think most of us give up and forget about such haunts early on in life. But I am haunted by something that happened to me while I served briefly on the mission field in Zaire. It occurred sometime around the fifth week of our stay there and I haven't been able to put it out of my mind yet. It bothers me. I've told my family and several of my friends about it. I'm struggling to know how to deal with it, to respond to it. I think about it at times when I'm getting ready to go to sleep at night, and even now, after a long time, I can't really make sense out of it. It's something quite outside my realm of experience. It haunts me.

With our images as they are about Africa, I can imagine that by now you are quite curious about my haunting experience there, but before I satisfy your curiosity, I'd like to share with you another story—one with which we're all familiar, one that I imagine has haunted very few of us.

Jesus was in Jerusalem teaching in the temple during the last week of his life. During his time there, Jesus went to the part of the temple known as the treasury and watched as people gave their offerings. While he was at the treasury, there was a steady flow of rich people coming in and donating large sums of money. After a while, an obviously poor woman came in and put two small copper coins into the offering. Seeing this, Jesus called to his followers and said, "Truly I tell you, this poor widow has put in more than all those who are contributing to the treasury. For all of them have contributed out of their abundance; but she out of her poverty has put in everything she had, all she had to live on" (Mark 12:43–44).

Ask yourselves, truthfully now, has that story ever haunted you? Is it one that you often think about, that you can't get out of your mind? Do you struggle with how to respond to it? Does it affect your living day-to-day? Probably not.

Back to Zaire. Bokeke was our night guard. He is a small, wiry man with a grin as wide as the great Zaire River itself. Our students at the seminar assured us, *"il est feroce, il est vraiment dangereux."* (He's ferocious, he's very dangerous!) That was a good reputation for our night guard to have, but our experience of Bokeke was that he is a life-loving, kindhearted man. Bokeke is also very poor, as are most of the people of Zaire. Though we did not witness starvation in that country, there were many, many hungry people there. The average diet consists of one meal a day of manioc leaves and roots. Fish might be thrown in on special occasions, as might be rice or beans. The average salary for a Zairean worker was about five hundred Zaires per month. Five hundred Zs was worth a little less than ten U.S. dollars, and it is that amount that supports most Zairean families. As I said, Bokeke is very poor.

My husband David and I struggled with the idea of having people work for us. In some ways, it seemed colonistic, almost patronizing, to hire people to work in our home but, at the same time that it seemed wrong, we also knew that by providing a job where previously there hadn't been one, we would help someone in need. Anyway, we needed the hired help. Perhaps the most difficult thing about the whole situation was that in hiring Bokeke we realized just how wealthy we really are in comparison to his poverty. Our salary for one month, though modest by U.S. standards, was more than most of our Zairean friends would make in fifteen years.

You can imagine, then, how I felt when on a rainy night, a chilly 78 degrees—chilly by Zairean standards!—I was able to give Bokeke my bright red NEBRASKA sweatshirt. Bokeke was thrilled. New clothes are few and far between for him, and a deep giggle, which came from the depths of his soul, rose up out on the back porch as I closed the door and returned to bed. I certainly couldn't foresee a time that I would ever feel cold in Zaire, and it felt marvelous to be able to give that shirt to Bokeke and have it make him so happy. You can also imagine with me how good it felt to be able to share part of our food with Bokeke. Often I would fix more dinner than David and I could really eat and so, since we didn't have a refrigerator, we saved it to give to Bokeke when he came to work. Several times, when we gave him part of our meal, that same giggle could be heard as he crossed the backyard on his way to his shelter.

One morning, the Sunday after David came down with the malaria that eventually caused us to come home, I decided to make cinnamon muffins for breakfast. As Bokeke was getting ready to go home for the day, I called him up to the house and gave him several of the muffins and some fruit and told him, "Have a happy Sunday, Bokeke." David was feeling a little better that day and it felt good to be able to share something a little special with Bokeke.

Now comes the part of the story that haunts me. That evening Bokeke arrived just before sundown and came to the door with his smile spread wide across his face. From behind his back he gave me a large package of sorts and said, "Happy Sunday, Mama!" In that package first of all was a great big fresh pineapple. In a separate pouch were about ten sweet potatoes, and, finally, wrapped up ever so carefully in a manioc leaf were four chicken eggs. "Happy Sunday, Mama!" Here was Bokeke, a man who had next to nothing, giving what would have been worth almost half of his month's income to us. "Happy Sunday, Mama!" It haunts me.

"Then he called his disciples and said to them, 'Truly I tell you, this poor widow has put in more than all those who are contributing to the treasury. For all of them have contributed out of their abundance; but she out of her poverty has put in everything she had, all she had to live on.'" It haunts me.

I'd like to tell you another story, one we're all familiar with. I don't know if it ever haunts you or not. It is this: Jesus gave his life, on a cross, for us. It haunts me.

Why? It haunts me because I live in a society where "looking out for number one" is the slogan, where "live and let live" is the rule. A society where people quote, "Am I my brother's keeper?" and think that the answer is "no." I live in a society where most think a dollar or two given to some cause is contributing to charity. I am haunted because even in our churches, where we claim to have accepted Christ's gift of new life, we often live as though we haven't.

Why do the stories of the widow and Bokeke haunt me? Because in them I recognize myself as one who gives out of plenty, and in the widow and Bokeke I come to know Jesus Christ who gave his everything for me and for us all. I am haunted because I'm not sure how to respond—the need is great and I feel so small. I am haunted because I am scared to respond, scared of the responsibility—and yet I know I must. Have you ever felt that way? Haunted?

I never told you the end of the story about Bokeke that Sunday morning. After he had given me the pineapple, potatoes, and eggs, and after he said, "Happy Sunday, Mama!" he turned, and as he was heading back to his shelter at the edge of our yard, I saw his grin, wide as the great Zaire River itself, and heard that giggle welling up as if from the center of the earth itself.

If God empowers the poorest of the poor in this world to be cheerful and loving givers, surely God will also empower us to be the same. Amen.

"𝒴es, Lord!"

Lydia Land

> **Lydia Land** is currently minister of Christian
> education at First Christian Church in Marion,
> Indiana. She is a graduate of Atlantic Christian
> College and Christian Theological Seminary. Lydia
> is a third-generation Disciple and the first
> "Priscilla" (not "Timothy") of Broad Street
> Christian Church in New Bern, North Carolina.

Mark 6:30–44

Thanksgiving Day is once again at hand. It's that time of the year when we take a glimpse of the world that reaches to the heart of humanity. It is especially a time to look at what Thanksgiving is all about. Pictures of our brothers and sisters in this world, and the life we share, flicker in front of us. You can see them in your mind, if you try. Come with me, and see....

Don and Julie are expecting their first baby. Don is sleeping on the couch as a lazy Saturday progresses away. Julie, however, notices that, well, this is the ninth month and her due date was last week. Julie waddles in her pregnant state over to Don. "Wake, honey," she says, "it's time." For a split second, Don's eyes flash open. Then he jumps up from the couch, dashes past Julie, trips over the coffee table, throws open the closet doors, puts one arm in the sleeve of his coat, grabs Julie's coat, places it on her shoulders, grabs the suitcase—"My keys! My keys! Where are my keys!?!" shouts Don. Meanwhile, Julie is chuckling between the labor spasms, as Don wildly goes about the apartment getting things ready to go to the hospital. She thinks to herself, "Now I know how Lucy felt when she told Ethel, Fred, and Ricky that she was going to have a baby."

Happy Thanksgiving, Julie, Don, and baby Zack!

The symbol of the wall was cold, marked with graffiti, and had been a deadly barrier to over eighty-three people who had tried to climb it in search of freedom. The wall was also a barrier to the East German citizens in general, keeping them in check within a country holding its citizens against their will. In the wake of the media, the wall has come a-tumbling down. East Germans have boarded trains and today can climb the wall and not be shot. West Germans have greeted their fellow East Germans with love and added hope in being reunited.

Glücklich Thanksgiving, Deutchland!

Hurricanes, earthquakes, tornadoes...it's as if nature has lashed out its fury against humanity, but humanity has shown how peace and kindness and love can comfort and give hope to others who have experienced these natural disasters. I'll never forget the despair I felt in trying to reach Rev. Amarylis Alverado in Puerto Rico as reports came in about the damage of Hurricane Hugo. Finally an answer...*"Buenas Noches!" "Buenas Noches,* Amarylis, this is Lydia!" I said. And laughter with tears could be heard from the other end of the telephone line. "Tell your people at Northview Christian Church, tell your people that in the name of our Lord Jesus, they have blessed us with their prayers. Everyone is OK. Tell them thank you, thank you, thank you!"

Happy Thanksgiving, Rev. Amarylis and Peso Ciales Christian Church!

Marge and Harriet are elderly sisters who are shut-ins, the only ones left in their family. Thanksgiving is a time when they are dependent upon others. They sit in their chairs a bit subdued. "They'll be here soon," Marge reassures Harriet. Beep! Beep! In walk the Joneses. They're from the church, and they've volunteered to deliver Thanksgiving dinners today to those in need. Bob walks in, "Miss Marge, Miss Harriet, we have your Thanksgiving dinner here, and we got our dinners as well. May we join you for about an hour or so and celebrate Thanksgiving with you?" Harriet's eyes twinkle. "Why, Bob and Mary, we wouldn't have it any other way!"

Happy Thanksgiving, Marge, Harriet, and the Joneses!

Five Jesuit priests killed in San Salvador...terrorist holding hostages in the Middle East...an environment being carelessly destroyed at the hands of its caretakers...the poor...the hungry...drug addicts...drug dealers...latchkey kids...abused children...abortion...churches losing people...separated families...greedy stockbrokers...take the money and run...babies with AIDS...frozen embryos...consumerism... sexism...murders...rapes...chaos in God's world.... Thanksgiving?

A carpenter goes to the boat, to a lonely place. He has been told that his cousin John has been murdered. Crowds surround him. They have heard about his teaching of God's love. And when he goes ashore, the crowd presses upon him. Tears well up in his eyes, and Jesus feels compassion for them and he heals their sick.

The disciples know it's getting late. "Jesus, this is a deserted, lonely place. Send the crowd away to go and get food for themselves."

We say that, too, in today's world. With a flip of the channel, a push on the button of the remote control, or throwing the special offering envelope in the trash can, we don't have to listen to the world's cries or see their tears and bloated bodies. We can isolate ourselves from all the chaos.

And Jesus says, "No, no, no. They need not go away. You feed them." We stumble and stammer in our faith. We reply, "But we only have five loaves and two fish. We are a small church. We have to limit our funds to ourselves. What can one person do?"

"Bring them here to me," Jesus says. He tells the crowd to sit down. And taking the two fish and five loaves, he looks up to heaven and blesses, breaks, and gives the loaves to the disciples, and the disciples give them to the crowd.

You know the ending of the story. They had more than enough for the five thousand. In fact, they took up twelve baskets full of crumbs.

God's thanksgiving wish is that when Jesus looks to us, individually or as his church, and says, "You give them something to eat," we will say without a bat of the eye, "Yes, Lord."

*E*yes to see

Eleanor Scott Myers

Eleanor Scott Myers is just entering her new
role as president of Pacific School of Religion,
Berkeley, California, after serving as academic
dean and professor of church and society at St. Paul
School of Theology in Kansas City, Missouri. Dr.
Myers holds degrees from Florida State University,
Yale University, and the University of Wisconsin.
She is currently one of nine theological consultants
across the nation working on the Project of
Globalization of Theological Education.

Matthew 22:1–4 and Psalm 115:1–11

Often my visceral reaction to hearing a parable from the gospel tradition is a contradictory one: "I don't really know what that story means...but I feel pretty certain that I won't like it!"

Indeed, these initial verses of Matthew 22 sound like a horror story. What begins in a joyful mood, with an invitation to a celebration, turns immediately into a tale of indifference, suspicion, and murder, followed by torture and death.

A very important person is inviting all those on the social register to a great wedding feast. But no one chooses to come. It is not just that they don't want to attend, however. The "regrets," the "sorry, I'm not available," become filled with violence. The invited ones go so far as to kill the ones who bring the invitation.

Then the person who is giving the party calls out troops and orders those who refused the invitation to be killed and the city where they live burned and totally destroyed. To complicate matters further, while that rampage goes on, the host tells other servants to go out on the street and bring in anyone they can find. Anyone and everyone winds up invited to the dinner party.

Well, there you have it. Perhaps before this text is read, we should flash one of those warning signs used on TV these days,

113

to indicate that what is coming might be too violent for the eyes and ears of children—not to mention adults. This is not the story of a wedding feast, we say. This is a horror story, a shocking tale.

But this story is a parable. This is a story that in its very telling is intended to be confusing. We don't understand it, but at the same time we know enough about what it might mean to be rather unsettled by it.

It is important to understand this parable within its context in Matthew's narrative. Jesus is in the midst of a series of hostile debates. His use of a parable to try to teach is a deliberate strategy, for it tends to catch people off guard and thereby perhaps more open to a new word—and to a transformation in the way they live their lives.

The confusion comes from the fact that there are two messages in the parable: one for those who are "blind and deaf" and one for those who can "see and hear." Different folks in the crowds that surrounded Jesus had different capacities to understand the word Jesus was sharing. Those who were discouraged—the dispossessed, the outcasts—could see through the parable and hear in it a word of hope from this teacher. However, those more privileged (and often life-denying) people could not readily understand Jesus' saving word of hope. For these who could not *see* (or hear!), there was a warning embedded in the story.

Jesus knew that social power and privilege grant persons the ability to distance themselves from the stark realities of life. These people in the crowd around Jesus just could not see, could not hear. They could not grasp the simple logic of the story because they did not understand or acknowledge their own need, their own despair. To these people in the crowd, the parable was a mystification, something they puzzled over or became angry about without knowing why. What Jesus hoped to do was to draw them, *unexpectedly*, into the story, to teach them "to see."

The social world in which the gospel event takes place is one in which there are large groups of people living without basic material needs, cut off from economic resources for well-being. And then there is a smaller elite group living in well-to-do material comfort. Many in this group are devoutly religious. Those who are "without" have begun to agitate, to confront the rich and powerful—who are fighting back, wanting to hold on to their privileged status. The hostilities surrounding the ministry of Jesus are born in this social strife.

Our task as participants of a would-be faithful community today is to try to hear the gospel, the word of God, in the midst of our own social strife, in order that we might be drawn toward a life together that helps usher in a time of fullness of life for everyone—including ourselves. Those of us who are well-fed and well-clothed, those of us who have lucrative work to do, are missing the point if we believe that what the gospel calls us to do is to try somehow to improve the lot of those who have less than we do. We fail to realize that we too stand among the discouraged, the disheartened. We too are those in need of the gospel word that would draw us back into life.

I do not know you, gathered here in this house of worship today, and yet I do know you: You...we...are that person who struggles against the fatal symptoms of heart disease and other illnesses related to stress. You...we...are the separated, the divorcing, the divorced, who know the pain of failed relationships and love's hopes surrendered. You...we...are one of those trapped in a nightmare of physical or psychological violence, probably hidden from public view. You...we...are struggling with alcoholism, drug and substance abuse, and a wasted physical and emotional life—whether our own or our child's, our spouse's, or our lover's. You...we...are the one who lives with deep disappointment that a child of ours seems off track and we feel helpless to alter the course. You...we...are the one whose parents are dying—or not dying physically but experiencing the uselessness of a worn-out body or scattered mind. You...we...are the one feeling abandoned and lost, by the death of a loved one, by the loss of a job. Need I go on?

The point is this: Until we who (by the world's standards) live privileged lives begin to acknowledge the pain, the separation, the lostness, the rootlessness in our own lives, we simply do not have "ears to hear, eyes to see" the word of God. We are unable to be parabled, unable to hear and grasp a way to turn our lives around—unable to learn to choose life instead of death.

Sallie McFague's work defines the way that seeing and believing lead us to work for new ways of being.[1] This begins with our imaginative participation—through one of Jesus' parables—in the contrast between what is and what might be. The gospel is very much about that contrast. This is what being parabled is about: An old familiar word or story is suddenly seen in a new setting because of some insight, and we suddenly find ourselves there in that familiar story but now with a new possibility. Something very ordinary, such as a story of an invitation to a celebration, becomes the moment for seeing and (hopefully) understanding something strange and extraordinary: Namely, that we, and everyone else too, receive what we don't deserve—and that it is important to be alert to the possibility of this gift so that it might change the way we live for ourselves and for others.

Worship begins. We hear the words of the text: "The kingdom of heaven may be compared to...." We sit back and relax. We are at church and here is a simile, an image that illustrates something we already know. Then suddenly we realize that we do not already know, really, what the kingdom or realm of heaven is! We are caught off guard—*if heaven is like that!*

This is a moment of vulnerability, for the story is unsettling; it is *not* reassuring. Then we are called to listen more carefully, and to remember. What we must remember is that Jesus not only tells shocking stories but leads a shocking life, which comes to a shocking end. And when we finally "see," we are invited and challenged to do the same. This is the way of faith, and when we walk in that faith, we do find joy and celebration as well as challenge and hard work. That, my friends, is the gospel.

McFague reminds us that, in a religious metaphor, what we learn is not primarily something about God but rather a new way to live ordinary life—our own.

Today our world cries out desperately for the ways of love and justice that are brought about by people who are not afraid to let their lives be disrupted, not afraid to be "parabled."

Today, through this text, I as a minister of the church invite you both to dis-ease and to the celebration of God's good news. A feast of goodness has been poured out for each and every one of us. In the setting of this feast, God hopes toward that day when we may have the courage to live faithfully, to love fully, and to be about the creating of just relationships—that God's reign might truly be in our midst.

---

[1]Sallie [TeSelle] McFague, *Speaking in Parables*. Fortress Press, 1975. I am indebted to her work on which this section of the sermon is based.

$\mathcal{B}$linded by a log

Marsha Bishop

Marsha Bishop is an associate regional
minister with the Christian Church (Disciples of
Christ) in Oklahoma, with primary responsibilities
for leadership development and Christian
education. A native Texan, she is a graduate of
Texas Christian University and Brite Divinity
School. "Blinded by a Log" was the first sermon
Marsha ever preached, in Hutchins, Texas.

Luke 6:39–45

A friend of mine who taught the first- and second-grade
Sunday school class at her church told me that she had been
talking with her class about prayer. They had been studying
examples of prayer in the Bible, and that Sunday the topic was
the story of the Pharisee who went up to the temple to pray
proclaiming, "God, I thank you that I am not like other people,"
contrasted with the tax collector who stood with bowed head
and said, "God, be merciful to me, a sinner" (Luke 18:11,13).

At the end of Sunday school, the class gathered in their
usual friendship circle. They went around the circle with each
child saying a sentence prayer: "Thank you, God, for the
beautiful day." "Thank you, God, for our family." "Thank you,
God, for our friends." "Thank you, God, for not making us like
those mean old Pharisees."

We shook our heads and smiled. Somehow or another, the
lesson obviously hadn't clicked. Perhaps they needed to grow a
little older to understand concepts like self-righteousness and
humility. I guess we didn't understand very well when we were
in the first grade either.

Like the story of the Pharisee and the tax collector, the
scripture we heard today is a familiar one. Most of us probably

117

learned it as children. Next to "Judge not, lest ye be judged," "Take the log out of your own eye before you try to take the speck out of your friend's eye" was my grandmother's stock comment when I started talking about someone's shortcomings. We know that we should get our own lives in order before we try to show others the way. And we have tried to do that, haven't we? But it's so much easier to recognize the speck in someone else's eye than it is to the see the log in our own.

This is a perplexing problem. We want to speak the word of God. We want to speak out on issues that we consider important to us and to our community. We study to learn how to help ourselves and our neighbor. And we truly know that our lives have been transformed by our faith. Yet there are times when we are anything but Christlike in our behavior and our attitude, times when our patience is really tried, times when it seems far easier to love our enemy than our neighbor and we just can't seem to control these feelings. When we see these attitudes in ourselves, it's not so easy to shake our heads and smile as my friend and I did at the children in the Sunday school class.

In spite of all our efforts, there are times when we are blinded by a log in our eye, a log that's not easy to remove. Since this particular log did not grow from a tree of sinful actions, at least not those of the Ten Commandment variety—lying, cheating, stealing, and so forth—neither apologies for doing something wrong nor any flurry of "good works" is likely to remove it.

Maybe we need to take a closer look at the log, if we really want to get it out. What is our log?

In today's scripture, Jesus prefaced his instruction to get the log out by addressing his hearers as, "You hypocrites"—not you thieves, you murderers, or you adulterers, but you *hypocrites*. Sometimes I wonder if I had been in that group of people listening to Jesus, if I might not have preferred to be called a thief. After all, Jesus was consistently compassionate in his attitude toward the outcasts of society: the thieves, the prostitutes, the tax collectors—all people who were prejudged by *what* they were.

Perhaps crying out, "You hypocrites!" was a very human cry of frustration at his listeners' inability to *see*. Earlier in this same chapter, Luke records two confrontations between Jesus and the religious leaders of the day, the Pharisees. The first was when Jesus happened to be walking through fields of grain and his disciples had plucked some ears, rubbed them between their palms, and eaten them—on a Sabbath. Later, the Pharisees were waiting in the synagogue for Jesus to break a Sabbath law. This time, he healed a man with a withered hand. The Pharisees were unable to see the good he did because they were blinded by the law he broke.

And these weren't the only occasions when Jesus was prejudged for what he was rather than who he was. When he read from the scripture and taught in his home synagogue, he was run out of town and barely escaped harm. So many people could only see *what* he was—that upstart carpenter's son from Nazareth who went around flaunting religious laws and tradition. They were blind to who he was.

Could it be that we are also hypocrites blinded by a log? Jesus teaches us to love our neighbor as ourselves, but do we always do that? Don't we sometimes feel smug and secure in our knowledge of what's "right"? Don't we sometimes look down our noses at someone who is different? We tend to put people into categories—teenagers, old folks, lazy, wild, liberal, conservative.

This is not to say that Jesus expected us always to be accepting and calm. We all know people who are irritating and some that are downright disgusting. We just wish they would see the light. These feelings aren't hypocritical, they are very real.

It's hypocritical when we try to mask in the appearance of love and good will things that we don't feel. It's hypocritical when we are so self-assured in the concepts *we* feel others should see, that we are blind to the light that is already there. It's hypocritical when we profess to love our neighbor, but make superficial judgments without seeking to know the real person. Sometimes we see *what* a person is before we find out *who* she or he is. Sometimes we look without seeing, listen without hearing, speak without meaning, and touch without feeling.

What is our log? I believe the essence of the log is judgment, intolerance, self-righteousness. Maybe it's simply that we feel very unloving toward those who are different, and we look down on those who are less than perfect or those of whose appearance, background, race, or profession we disapprove.

Unfortunately, identifying the log doesn't remove it. So how do we get rid of it once and for all?

Well, Jesus didn't just tell us to take the log out of our eye and leave us hanging without telling us how. If we will go back to the sentence before the instruction to take the log out of our eye, we find that he said, "A disciple is not above the teacher, but *everyone* who is fully qualified will be like the teacher" (Luke 6:40).

Be like the teacher.

Jesus, the teacher, is the model for both a view and a practice of life. In his book *On Being a Christian,* Hans Kung writes of the "sheer friendliness" of Jesus. He goes on to say that nowhere in the gospels is Jesus described in terms of his virtues. Far from it. It's always in terms of his actions and his relations with others. Jesus is our savior, not because he was a good man who did some miraculous things. He is our savior because he "did not regard equality with God as something to be exploited, but emptied himself, taking the form of a slave" (Philippians 2:6–7). He loved us enough to empty himself, pouring out his infinite love and taking our sins into himself that we might know eternal life.

And there's more. Jesus also says, "No good tree bears bad fruit, nor again does a bad tree bear good fruit" (Luke 6:43). We're so familiar with the verse, "You will know them by their fruits" (Matthew 7:16), that I think we often jump to the conclusion that fruits and good works are the same. But here, Jesus continues: "The good person out of the good treasure of the heart produces good...for it is out of the abundance of the heart that the mouth speaks" (Luke 6:45).

If we consider for a moment the fruit-bearing trees Jesus referred to, we'll realize that a plant doesn't just "bear fruit." Plants are continually growing—or dying. And there's a lot of work involved before a plant bears fruit. The soil must be prepared. It needs water, sunshine, fertilizer, weeding.

A few years ago, I planted a vegetable garden and learned firsthand what is involved in making a plant bear fruit. Most of you know far better than I.

One of the vegetables I wanted to grow a lot of was okra. Now I know anyone who is not from the southern part of the country (and probably many who are) would wonder why anyone would deliberately grow that slimy little vegetable. But for those of us who have grown up munching on fried okra or enjoying a steaming bowl of gumbo, okra is indeed a delicacy.

But, though I have undoubtedly consumed bushels of okra in my lifetime, I had never laid eyes on an okra plant. Much to my surprise, okra is a tall plant and each one produces a lot of okra. Another thing I learned about okra is that you have to pick it every day. It grows so fast that almost overnight the okra pods are large and woody—not worth eating. The okra, if not picked, quickly turns its attention inward. It stops producing new fruit and concentrates on perpetuating itself by turning the fruit into hard, log-like seed pods. Needless to say, I picked every day and our entire neighborhood feasted on okra.

Oh yes, another thing about okra—as it gets larger, it gets prickly. It has at the base of the fruit little spines, almost like miniature cactus quills, that hurt your fingers when you try to pick it.

Though Jesus never mentioned okra, I think he may have had something similar in mind. Like the okra, we must be cultivated and fed until our lives are transformed and we begin to produce good fruit.

But it doesn't stop there. We must pick the fruit and give it away in love or, like the okra, we too will stop producing and turn our attention inward, becoming *self*-centered and concentrating on perpetuating ourselves, hardening our attitudes until our fruit also becomes woody and log-like. Our fruit is no longer worth eating and if one would partake of it, she would find it prickly. It hurts the hands of those who reach out to touch it.

You see, we don't just take the log out of our eye once, we take it out every day. Like the plant, our lives too must be continually growing, the weeds continually pulled, the log continually removed from our eye. That's the nature of the way we are.

If our lives have been transformed by our faith, that is only the beginning. We must pick the fruit of love and good will every day, for it is only in the giving that we continue growing and producing good fruit abundantly. And, in imitation of our teacher, we learn to give it away in "sheer friendliness." Then we too, "out of the good treasure of our heart, produce good, out of the abundance of our heart, the mouth speaks."

The scripture doesn't really focus on the log in our own eye but on *removing* it, so that we may see more clearly to help our brothers and sisters with the speck.

When my children were still preschoolers, I drove a route regularly for Meals on Wheels. It was primarily in a housing project in Dallas and I usually got a sitter for the boys. One day the sitter didn't show up so I had to take them with me. I scooped up several old magazines to take with us for the elderly people on the route and off we went. At first, the boys were a little frightened and hesitant to approach the strange places, but after several stops, they were enjoying themselves immensely.

There was one older woman on the route, though, who was a real pain in the neck. She had broken her hip and the experience had apparently soured her toward everything and everyone. She was a grouch. If there was nothing to complain about, she'd usually bark out, "Just put the meal in the refrigerator, I'll get to it later." I tried to talk with her once or twice, but she was so rude, it was hard to be nice. I hated to ruin the boys' morning by exposing them to her, but I was afraid to leave them alone in the car.

Garnett, who was five, picked up a couple of the magazines and said, "I'll bet she will really like a magazine." (Fat chance, I thought.) Then Andrew, who was only two and a half, wanted something to carry. I handed him the milk, but not satisfied, he stopped and picked a couple of dandelions on the way.

I knocked on the door. The cranky voice said, "You're late today. Come on in, it's unlocked." I opened the door and the boys pushed past me and ran to the woman. "We bought you some neat magazines, see?" Garnett fairly shouted.

"I brought something too," chirped Andrew, practically falling into her lap with his two bedraggled dandelions. I thought I'd better get them out before she started yelling at them or worse. I apologized for their rambunctious behavior. Garnett romped down the stairs, and I turned to take Andrew's hand. "Bye-bye," he said, waving. I glanced back at the woman. She had pulled herself up, clutching the two dandelions in the hand that held onto her walker and waving with the other. The bitter expression on her face had melted into a smile that brightened the tears rolling down her cheeks.

A log in your eye can really make you blind.

Giving birth to compassion

Marilyn W. Spry

Marilyn Spry is the new pastor of First Christian Church in Downers Grove, Illinois. A graduate of Lexington Theological Seminary, Marilyn has been a minister in the Christian Church (Disciples of Christ) for twenty -six years. This sermon was preached on the Sunday before Thanksgiving during her previous pastorate at Northside Christian Church in St. Louis, Missouri.

Matthew 25:31–46

Someday we want to hear Christ say to us, "Truly I tell you, just as you did it to one of the least of these who are members of my family, you did it to me" (Matthew 25:40). These powerful words from the Gospel of Matthew are part of a series of teachings by Jesus about "the end time." They are in the form of an "apocalyptic vision." This kind of speaking was not meant to provide details or a diagram about when, or how, the end of time would come. It was, instead, an ethical instruction that Jesus gave to his followers so that they might know what was really important to God. He wanted to be sure they knew how to live in the meantime.

Matthew places this teaching just before the passion of Jesus. It is the last thing that he said to his followers before his time of trial and death. It is much like what parents would do if they were to leave their children for awhile. They might have given many other words of instruction, but now they want to be sure that the children hear this so they will be fully prepared for their absence. No surprises!

Surprise, however, is an element of this scripture, both for those who served the least and those who didn't. They were *both* surprised about what was most important to God. Perhaps we

123

are not surprised by the words. After all, we have had many long years of experience in charitable works and are fully aware that much of the help that is given to needy people has come about by the example of the church. We have heard this before. But have we? While we may see ourselves as loving and giving to many people, it may surprise us that there are no qualifiers attached to "the least of these." Yes, we may be surprised, especially when we can hear ourselves wanting to limit our compassion to people we like or who show proper appreciation for our efforts, or people who are clean, pleasant, and deserving, or people who are innocent and have "really tried."

However, the word seems very clear. Is there anyone who does not understand the basis for judgment or the clear statement of what it is that pleases God? No, it is all too clear! The deeper question that troubles our hearts may be, "How do we become compassionate people with eyes that see only a person's need?

In his book *The Power of the Powerless,* Christopher de Vinck tells a simple story:

> One spring afternoon my five-year-old son, David, and I were planting raspberry bushes along the side of the garage....A neighbor joined us for a few moments....David pointed to the ground...."Look, Daddy! What's that?" I stopped talking with my neighbor and looked down. "A beetle," I said.

> David was impressed and pleased with the discovery of this fancy, colorful creature. My neighbor lifted his foot and stepped on the insect, giving his shoe an extra twist in the dirt. "That ought to do it," he laughed. David looked up at me, waiting for an explanation, a reason....That night, just before I turned off the light in his bedroom, David whispered, "I liked that beetle, Daddy." "I did too," I whispered back.[1]

Compassion eludes us, even for tiny, colorful creatures who are part of God's creation. Compassion eludes us, from beetles to human beings. Why is it that in even "good Christian hearts" there are so many blind spots—so much fear, prejudice, and selfishness? Why are our feet sometimes quicker than our hearts?

Sue Monk Kidd tells of her experience as a twelve-year-old that became a significant part of her spiritual journey toward compassion. She had gone to a nursing home with a youth group from her church. She was really there at her mother's insistence, because she had wanted to go with some friends from school to the swimming pool as the last fling of the summer. But her mother had not heard her pleas and so she found herself standing in front of an ancient-looking woman. Everything about her was sad. She had a worn face, a lopsided grin, and her gray hair was peeking out from under her crocheted lavender cap. Sue pushed the bouquet of crepe paper flowers toward the woman. The woman looked at her and Sue felt as if the woman's eyes were piercing deep inside of her. Then the woman spoke the words that Sue has never forgotten. "You didn't want to come, did you, child?" The words were too painful and too honest and she protested that indeed she really had wanted to come. And then a smile lifted one side of the old woman's mouth and she said, "It's OK, you can't force the heart."

That's it! You can't force compassion. It is a process. You don't just decide, "Now I will be compassionate." Certainly we can do kind deeds for people but with many motivations. Sometimes we act out of fear, guilt, or a sense of duty. While that may be the way we begin, God wants hearts that are moved to serve others by compassion.

It really should not be a surprise that the development of compassion is a process, for all of life is a process. In nature, first there is a seed, then a sprout, a blossom, and finally fruit. The larva nestles inside of a cocoon for a long time until it finally struggles forth as a beautiful butterfly. And think of the development of a human being that moves from an ovum to fetus, to a baby, then a child, an adolescent, and finally an adult.

Meister Eckhart, a fourteenth-century theologian and mystic, once said, "We are all meant to be mothers of God." Since God is love and all compassion, our purpose and identity as God's children is to have God's compassion born deeply in us. We are to be God's love on earth. When we open our hearts and choose to go on a journey of faith with Christ, we begin a journey that, along the way, transforms our hearts into compassionate places.

As a part of the process, we begin to move from thinking of *they* to thinking of *we*. As long as "the least" of these are nameless, faceless labels, they seem like foreigners and strangers. They may even seem threatening.

Rev. Larry Rice, a St. Louis minister and advocate for the homeless, tries in many ways to help us see those in need. He enlists people who are willing to share part of the Christmas Day to go and help serve dinner to the homeless in the community. He also has written a booklet entitled "As the Giant Sleeps, the People Suffer." He has shared it with many churches in the area. In it he shares the stories and words of many homeless people and begins to give them faces. Look at this face:

> Living on the streets can be painful. You aren't able to wash your body and it is hard to keep warm. You don't know what it is like to leave school at the end of the day, not knowing where you are going to sleep tonight—it's so hard. I have three brothers and sisters and a lovely mother. My father died when I was five years old.
>
> *Lisa (age 9)*

Recently, I went to the city jail where the seminary supervision case conference was to be held. Two students were doing field education there. Julie, a mid-life seminarian, told of visiting with a thirty-nine-year-old prisoner. He was educated, had a good job, and was married and the father of four children. He had gotten involved with drugs and was awaiting his trial. In many ways, the two of them were worlds apart. Then he began to tell about his new baby daughter whom he had never seen. He had only heard her cry on the phone. Tears came to his eyes as he talked about this tiny little life, his desire to get out and to be with his family, and to get right with God and the world. Julie felt her own tears as she listened to him. She was away from her family for several months as she began her seminary education. She had a two-year-old grandchild that she hadn't seen in five months. She knew the pain of loneliness and separation from family. In that moment of human sharing, she realized that in many ways, she and the prisoner were very much alike.

So often our unchanged hearts ask the old question "Am I my brother's keeper?" It is when we begin to see and hear with the eyes and ears of Christ that we begin to know that we are *one* with our brother, our sister. We begin to feel our oneness and interrelatedness with every creature of God, from beetle to human being. We begin to understand the words of the character Celie in the book *The Color Purple* when she says, "I know if I cut a tree, my arm would bleed."

To live with compassion means literally "to suffer with." When we suffer with and serve those in need, it is then that we understand that we are one. We begin to find that we are receiving gifts from them and are being enriched in ways we never dreamed. The compassion we need comes as we journey with Jesus Christ and follow in his way.

---

[1]Christopher de Vinck, *The Power of the Powerless: A Brother's Lesson*. Doubleday, 1988.

$\mathcal{T}$he simple covenant

M. Margaret Harrison

Margaret Harrison serves as regional minister and president of the Christian Church (Disciples of Christ) in the Southwest, the only woman presently occupying such a position. A native of Oklahoma, she is a graduate of Chapman College and Pacific School of Religion, and is a candidate in the D.Min. program at Brite Divinity School. This sermon was preached at University Christian Church in Fort Worth, Texas.

Luke 12:13–21

Did you hear those two stories? The ones that told of the Lukan Jesus and his concern for our welfare as we relate to our possessions? You say, "Oh, no! She's going to talk about possessions." Not so. I wish to speak about human nature.

In the first story, Jesus is asked to assume a role often taken by the rabbis of his time—that of arbitrator and judge—to decide about a disputed inheritance. He rejects that authority and continues to teach that *his* family is identified as those who listen to the word and act upon that word toward others. He denies that the things of this world have any real part in God's kingdom when he speaks about the danger of greed in any of its forms—even the settling of an inheritance.

The first story sets the stage for the second story, which becomes a commentary on greed. It tells how the *only* thing that the rich farmer could decide to do with his vast wealth was to increase the storage space to accommodate more of that accumulation. The story draws us up short with the description of the immensity of his wealth, followed immediately by the death of the landowner. Death—the common denominator for us all.

The question about death puts in perspective the fact of possessions: "Now who will get all that *you* have prepared?" The rich farmer, called a fool, symbolizes all of humanity that is seduced by greed in any form. The story, then, is about fools who have given themselves over to the task of preparing for a life of ease and security: those who have declared that there is no God by virtue of having given no thought to the provider of life itself and a relationship to that lifegiver. Nor have they given any thought to the *purpose* for living. For the amassing of fortunes, comfort, security—even power—becomes a single-minded purpose that takes on a life of its own and will *possess* us.

We may not be talking just about material possessions, for greed can spill over into all parts of life. I travel some. The airline magazines offer a look at the world I would probably otherwise miss. Recently, I was drawn to an article about Martha Stewart, who has built a lucrative business out of the art of hospitality. She teaches how to entertain by using simple, yet elegant, decoration and food selection. I thought that was both revolutionary and innovative in a time of opulence until I read further.

The article described her popular writing and video shows and then spoke of her motivation: She wants simply to be recognized by those whose opinions matter—e.g., society editors and the like—as an expert, as the best. She has spent years now developing her style and her image.

Not many months ago, she was party to an ugly divorce—a death-like event. How ironic! One who espouses hospitality had lost the art of hospitality, for there was no longer room for the most significant relations she had contracted, her marriage. Her quest for recognition and self-esteem had taken over her ability to live life. A very subtle—yet present—form of greed.

Truly, what concerns me is how far we human beings wander from our spiritual center: that relationship in which we are called by God to become God's people through our baptism into Christ. It's a simple covenant: I will be your God; you will be my people. That spiritual center is so easily replaced with one that focuses on ourselves and our abilities to amass wealth and control its uses. God seems to disappear.

The critical question is asked in our story today: "What shall I do?" The fool said, "Build bigger barns!" The spiritual *requirement* is to give our possessions away for others' sake. Calvin says we need to learn to live each day asking for our daily bread. That's the basis of the simple covenant: *trust*, that God will provide what we need because of God's care for us and God's promises to us.

If we read a little further in this chapter of Luke, we find that these two stories are prelude to that beautiful treatise on anxiety: Consider the lilies of the fields, the birds of the air. They toil not, neither do they spin. Yet they are arrayed in beauty. How much God cares for them and for us. (Luke 12:24–27.)

What a *deeply* rooted way to live! How wonderful not to be concerned about the future and what might happen, or not to be always hedging against inflation in order to continue to live in the manner to which we have become accustomed. How wonderful not to be anxious that we might not provide enough to ensure our security. Rather, how wonderful to become truly the agent of God's grace by opening ourselves to the stranger, the helpless, the needy. That does not mean that we should not work hard and be prudent about our possessions. It requires that we make *responsible decisions* about their use.

That is what it means to be God's people: to be so shaped by that love from God that we act out of *concern for others*. When we receive the mercy and blessing of God, the requirement is to pass it on as God's mercy. With the blessing of wealth comes the requirement to pass it on as God's blessing.

You say: I am only one, and the problems of the world are so great—I just can't be effective. Wait! *Whose* grace and mercy and resource are we working with? Or is it true that God does not exist?

We've all heard of the concerns of the environmentalists about our "disposable" waste, including diapers and Styrofoam. At the last General Assembly, I met a woman on the elevator carrying a ceramic cup filled with her morning coffee. I commented on her having her own cup. She remarked that it was her answer to Styrofoam and plastics.

How prophetic! One individual raising the consciousness of those she meets, including the fast-food vendors, by carrying her own cup. A measure of the grace of God toward our future generations? I find it so.

Now, don't hear me wrong: I am not trying to induce guilt about having our possessions. I am talking about not becoming involved in the inevitable chase after *things*. It's the *chase* that distracts us.

And I am talking about not *worrying* about our future. Death for all of us, whether our own or someone else's, should remind us that the future is not the question: It is the present that has meaning because of how we live. Is God a part of that and part of our motivation, or are we foolish about things?

In Psalm 28, the psalmist cries out for us, reminding us that no matter how far we wander from God as the center of our existence, God is there. "O Lord...my rock...protect your people"—because they are your people. The message is to us moderns, for we seem to have forgotten that we can repent— change direction and return to God—with a simple address. Again and again we can avail ourselves of the eternal promises of our faith.

Let us pray: Great and wonderful God, continue to draw us back to you and to bless us for your purposes in this world. Amen.

*R*eal humility, real faithfulness, real stewardship

LaTaunya M. Bynum

LaTaunya Bynum is a member of the staff of the Division of Homeland Ministries of the Christian Church (Disciples of Christ), serving as director of women in ministry. Her responsibilities include the nurture, advocacy, and support of Disciples clergywomen and ministerial candidates. Toni is a graduate of Chapman College and the School of Theology at Claremont.

Isaiah 58:1-9 and Matthew 5:13-16

Among the hymns we sing from time to time is one that invites us to proclaim our call and commitment to ministry. It is a hymn that speaks of that relationship between a person and God, and it speaks to me of the confession I made when I said several years ago, "Yes, I believe Jesus is the Christ, the Son of the living God." It is a confession I renewed when I was ordained, and it is a confession all of us are invited to renew from time to time. That hymn I hear some congregations singing even now is:

A charge to keep I have, A God to glorify;
A never-dying soul to save, And fit it for the sky.

That song reminds me that as important, unique, and gifted as I may be, I am not the center of all that is. The center is the God who is our creator, sustainer, and redeemer and has granted to all of us the responsibility of a steward. All of us are charged to keep some things for God. We keep our faith, our bodies, our minds, our souls.

How humbling to think that God knows and loves every one of us. How marvelous that God continues to hold out to us the opportunity to receive love and grace sufficient for all that we need.

When we give the allegiance of our hearts and our minds, our bodies and our souls to God, we are being faithful. The problem is that sometimes we confuse the form of faithfulness with the substance of faith. Sometimes we know what to do, but we forget why we do it. Even those of us who are called, blessed, hands laid on, set aside, know exactly what to do in our ministries, but we are sometimes hard-pressed to say why we do it.

It is not that we are overly arrogant, unusually willful, or deliberately disobedient. We just forget sometimes. We forget that the good news of Jesus Christ—hinted at in the prophets, proclaimed in the gospels, and expanded upon in the epistles—is the good news that challenges us always to see the reality before us and to live as if God's people matter.

Several years ago, historian Barbara Tuchman wrote a book called *A Distant Mirror*. She suggests that if we could hold up the history of the fourteenth century as if it were a mirror, we would see reflected back at us our own time in history. The parallels are clear:

Then as now, there were wars and rumors of wars among people in all parts of the world. The cold war may be ended, the Berlin Wall may be torn down, Nelsen Mandela may be out of jail and we praise God for that. But caution dictates that we not cry, "Peace, peace when there is no peace." Peace is not yet here, not in the Middle East, not in the British Isles, not in Central and South America, not even in North America.

Then as now, a growing middle class enjoyed great comfort and prosperity while other citizens lived in unhealthy and unsafe poverty.

Then as now, children were too often seen as prized possessions but not always as precious human beings worthy of our respect, our protection, and our love.

Then as now, there were killing diseases and panic born of fear and ignorance that too often led and leads to the harm of the sick person rather than to their health and healing.

Then as now, the church stood in the breach between life and death.

Both the prophet Isaiah and the gospel writer Matthew challenge us to be stewards of our spiritual and worship life. They challenge us to remember that only worship that is reflective of service and community in God's name will truly satisfy God.

As Isaiah wrote, the Jewish community had been exiled, their property confiscated, their leaders arrested, their lives utterly destroyed. Now they had returned from Babylon and were back in Judah trying to rebuild their lives. They built homes, they established a government, they began to worship. But something wasn't quite right, for even as they worshiped, they no longer understood the link between the ritual of worship and how to live out the worship they proclaimed.

These folks really were like us. They knew, for instance, that fasting was good, but while they were exiled, they forgot why, and because their motivation was gone, God did not respond to them as they thought God would. "We got the form right," we can almost hear them saying. "Why hasn't God paid attention to us?"

We hear their cry as our own. We do the right things. We come to church, pay tithes and offerings, train leaders, teach church school, sing in the choir, attend the meetings. Still, God does not respond as we think God should. Why is God not answering us?

Here's why—and remember, we are looking at ourselves as if in a mirror. The folks fasted and prayed. But like us sometimes, even as they prayed and went without food, they were abusing the ritual because their fasting was not to honor God but merely to accomplish the act. God was not the focus; *they* were.

They were practicing an empty ritual, filled with false humility, "Look, God, we are being humble now. Aren't we righteous?" They could not be faithful. And their fasting had no bearing on their lives.

But hear God say through the prophet: You have this fasting down to a science. You have the right brand of sackcloth, the right number of days without food, the right look of gauntness. But while you fast—maybe because hunger makes you irritable—you quarrel and fight with each other. While you fast, you abuse and exploit the folks who worked for you. You are a people whose history includes slavery, homelessness, deliverance, prosperity, exile, and restoration. How dare you oppress or exploit anybody. That is not acceptable.

What I want from you is a fast that serves humanity and honors God. What I want from you is a stewardship of faith. If you are bound by wickedness, get loose. If you know people who are enslaved by anything or anyone, even if it's you who are enslaved/the enslaver, set them or yourself free. If you know of oppression anywhere, be active in its elimination. If you have bread enough for you and you see hungry people, feed them. If you see someone in need of clothing, clothe them. If you know where any homeless people are, shelter them.

Our response tends to be: But God, this is a hard saying. People need boundaries and responsibility. We don't want to be taken advantage of. We don't want to be trapped. Rescuing people all the time is not good for them or us. This is the real world, where it is tough—and only the fittest, the strongest, the smartest, and the most privileged survive. I pulled myself up and out of the muck and mire of life, why can't they?

But God counters with another question: "Is not this the fast that I choose?" (Isaiah 58:6). The fast God calls us to is the fast from bad and broken relationships. It is a call really not just to a fast but to the feat of partnership with God and all of creation. To whatever extent we have material and professional success, we thank God. To whatever extent we struggle to make ends meet, to raise healthy children, to make a safe home, we ask God's guidance. To whatever extent we know the intimate love of another, we praise God for the gift of life-giving love.

And for those who see God's blessings in the mere fact that they are able to survive this day and who have not and may not ever know all of the blessings you know or I know, our truest fast, our truest worship of God, comes as all of us share all of our blessings together.

When we are true stewards, we will be blessed stewards. *The Good News Bible* describes the blessing this way: "Then my favor will shine on you like the morning sun, and your wounds will be quickly healed. I will always be with you to save you; my presence will protect you on every side. When you pray, I will answer you. When you call to me, I will respond" (Isaiah 58:8–9, TEV).

God will be there for us. That is a promise made to us, kept for us; Jesus died for it and God raised him up for it. Friends, that is the good news of Jesus Christ.

It is living as if that promise is true that makes us worthy of the words Jesus spoke: "You are the salt of the earth....You are the light of the world" (Matthew 5:13a, 14a).

We know about light, but what is this business about salt? In the ancient world, salt was one of life's necessities. It was a preservative, and it was believed to have had even some religious value. Salt was essential to life...in those days.

Jesus is saying to his disciples then and to us now, "You may not have everything, but you are not without power. You have a kind of power that is patient, persevering, but never, ever, passive. You can, by faith and courage, make things happen. You are valuable. You are alive. You are God's. Be the church of Jesus Christ.

In 1966, Martin Luther King, Jr., spoke at the Disciples' International Convention, which is the predecessor to the General Assembly. At that convention, Dr. King spoke words that all these years later are still true.

> If the church does not recapture its prophetic zeal, it will become little more than an irrelevant social club with a thin veneer of rigidosity. If the church does not partici- pate in the struggle for economic and racial justice, it will forfeit the loyalty of millions and cause people everywhere to say it has atrophied its will.

God has invited us into a church that is atrophied, its muscles limp and useless from lack of use. God calls us to be an active church, an alive and faithful and fit church. It is an active church that with others marched from Selma to Montgomery, broke down the Berlin Wall, opened a prison door in South Africa. When we have a portion of that unquenchable spirit for freedom, then we truly worship, then we are truly faithful, then we are truly salt and light. We are God's people.

We can endure anything, even when our souls feel sick and weary. We know we are not alone—God is with us.

Let it be so.

$\mathcal{B}$ridges to life

Allene M. Parker

Allene Parker serves as co-pastor of Peace
United Church of Christ in Tilden, Nebraska, with
her husband. She is a graduate of the School of
Theology at Claremont and San Francisco State
University. An earlier version of "Bridges to
Life" was preached in Berkeley, California,
inspired in part by the fiftieth anniversary
celebrations for the Oakland-Bay and
Golden Gate Bridges.

Deuteronomy 30:11–20; Amos 5:14; and Matthew 5:43–48

In his novel *The Fall,* Albert Camus tells the story of a man
who spends his life sitting in a bar at the center of Amsterdam,
commenting on life as he observes it happening around him.
Early in the story, this man, Jean-Baptiste, makes a comment
about the canals and bridges found in Amsterdam. His comment reveals much about his own nature, but also speaks
beyond himself:

> I never cross a bridge at night.... Suppose, after all, that
> someone should jump in the water. One of two things—
> either you do likewise to fish him out, and in cold
> weather, you run a great risk! Or you forsake him there
> and suppressed dives sometimes leave one strangely
> aching.[1]

Camus' character has a problem: He is afraid. And just what
is he afraid of? Does he fear crossing bridges? Diving into cold
water? Not really. His comments reveal that his real fear is of
getting involved, even by chance, in any situation where he
might have to make a choice, where he might have to become
personally involved in risk taking—particularly a situation
implied by the condition of night, where one cannot see through

137

the darkness to identify who jumped or whether or not it is safe for a would-be rescuer to dive. So he devises a perfectly logical solution: He never crosses bridges at night. However, it's not all that simple. The irony in this solution is that it is very difficult to move far in Amsterdam, in any direction, without crossing bridges. As some of you may know, the city of Amsterdam is built around a network of canals that spread out in circles like wheels, with spokes connecting them to the center. For Jean-Baptiste, secure in his cocoon at the center of his universe, his refusal to cross bridges at night translates into the reality that he goes nowhere at all, day or night. He takes no risks, and lives only vicariously through the lives of those others he observes and to whom he preaches his gospel of security.

Today I want to talk about bridges and choices and risk taking. Camus' story speaks to me because I suspect that there is a bit of Jean-Baptiste in each one of us, whether or not we are willing to admit it. We can understand his fear and his reluctance to take risks. Certainly we all know about feeling helpless in the face of unexpected events. We know about the cold chills down the spine, the knot in the stomach, the splitting headache, the nagging voice of guilt—those things that seem to correspond to our struggles to make the "perfect decision" that we fear may appear later on to be anything but perfect. So we struggle ahead in our lives from one crisis to the next. If things get really bad, why then we can always "burn our bridges behind us" (cutting off roads leading back to past places, people, and events) or "cross the next bridge as we come to it" (meaning we hope we can deal with the next crisis when it happens without worrying about future events).

Yes, like Jean-Baptiste, all of us know about bridges!

Webster defines a bridge as "a structure built over a depression or obstacle for use as a passageway."[2] As such, bridges are vital to the commerce, communication, and transportation needs of our society—especially in this particular part of the world where we depend on bridges to span the waterways dividing this sprawling urban area. The San Francisco Bay area is not Amsterdam—but for many of us, crossing bridges has become part of our daily routine. To get from here to there, we must cross the Oakland-Bay Bridge, the Golden Gate Bridge, or even the Richmond-San Rafael Bridge—to name just three. We recognized our dependence on these bridges in 1987 when we celebrated the fiftieth anniversaries for the Golden Gate and Oakland-Bay Bridges. This dependence became painfully apparent following the earthquake in October, 1989: With the Oakland-Bay Bridge out of service for a month, this routine commute that many took for granted became anything but routine! We were reminded of how bridges connect our cities, our jobs, and our busy lives: Even when traffic slows to a crawl over the bridges during peak commuting hours and tempers and radiators approach the boiling point, these bridges stand as visible, powerful symbols of connection.

Webster, in true scientific tradition, limits his definition of bridges to those physical characteristics that can be seen, touched, and measured. But there is another kind of bridge that is vital to our lives, a bridge of spirit and love that connects us to each other in relationship. This kind of bridge is invisible, yet it is strong enough to weather great storms. It reaches out to connect over the depressions and obstacles in our lives. It is a passageway for energy, communication, and the constructive employment of our ideas and talents.

When we reach out to each other, even from points of apparent weakness or vulnerability; when we care enough about our neighbors to take time to make their acquaintance and journey with them; when we are willing to risk building bridges of love and hope even in places where the loud voices of tradition would convince us that nothing constructive can be accomplished with the investment of our energies—then we are able to move closer to making peace and justice in our real world.

We all know that the problems facing our world are vast and overwhelming—so much so that often we do not agree among ourselves on what the problems are or how best to solve them. As Christian people, we may feel that our churches should be doing more to make our concerns present in the form of action. But we also realize how difficult it is to go that extra mile and put our time, energy, hearts, or money where our mouths are! Yet, if we truly want to be bridge builders, working to overcome the obstacles preventing us from living in a more peaceful and just world, we have to start somewhere.

The first scripture passage read to us this morning may provide us with that starting point. In Deuteronomy 30, Moses speaks to the people of Israel for the last time. The Israelites have wandered in the desert for forty years and their leader, Moses, is an old man near death. After so many years of struggle, they are on the verge of crossing over the river Jordan into the promised land of Canaan. As Moses begins to speak to the people, I imagine that many were anxious and impatient to "hit the road" and move on to the new experiences awaiting beyond the river. There were homes to build, crops to tend, cities to invade—plenty of excitement to anticipate! I can see the crowd of people listening to Moses that day. The sun is hot, throats are dry and dusty, babies are cranky, grown-ups are restless—and Moses stands up and begins to recite again, blow by blow, the long, *long* history of their wandering in the desert— nothing new and exciting there after all this time! The story is old and too familiar, belonging to an older generation. The people are eager to burn those bridges and cross the Jordan. Finally, Moses comes to the end of his speech, but he doesn't exactly send them forth with a benediction. Surely after forty years, a benediction would seem appropriate. Instead, Moses issues a new challenge—a challenge from God who had preserved them even in their wanderings. Hear again part of this challenge:

> I call heaven and earth to witness against you today that
> I have set before you life and death, blessings and curses.
> Choose life so that you and your descendants may live.
> *Deuteronomy 30:19*

To choose life is to make a decision to love God and walk in God's ways. Such a choice requires living a life of commitment and action that witnesses to God's loving concern for all God's creatures, no matter who they are or where they are.

In the eighth century B.C., the prophet Amos is called by God to leave his sheep and his orchard behind in the Judean countryside and to go up to the corrupt cities of Israel to proclaim the word of the Lord. Amos is sent to proclaim Israel's sins and impending doom. If you read the book of Amos carefully, you may discover that he still has quite a bit to say! Those evil cities in the eighth century B.C. don't sound a whole lot different than what we see on the evening news everyday in our twentieth-century living rooms. The prophet's plea that justice roll on like an ever-flowing river and righteousness like an ever-flowing stream (Amos 5:24) still needs to be heard and taken seriously. However, this message is not entirely gloom and doom. He offers hope as well, in the form of another challenge:

> Seek good and not evil, that you may live; and so the
> LORD, the God of hosts, will be with you, just as you have
> said.
> *Amos 5:14*

Eight centuries later, Jesus added a new dimension to the challenges set forth in the Mosaic law and the writings of the prophets:

> You have heard that it was said, "You shall love your neighbor and hate your enemy." But I say to you, Love your enemies and pray for those who persecute you, so that you may be children of your Father in heaven; for he makes his sun rise on the evil and on the good, and sends rain on the righteous and on the unrighteous. For if you love those who love you, what reward do you have? Do not even the tax collectors do the same? And if you greet only your brothers and sisters, what more are you doing than others? Do not even the Gentiles do the same? Be perfect, therefore, as your heavenly Father is perfect.
>
> *Matthew 5:43–48*

As God's children, we are to love each other, but that love is to extend beyond the comfort and security of our immediate loved ones—even to those we call enemies. That kind of love is risky and dangerous. It demands involvement in life to the point of willingness to risk what Jean-Baptiste in Camus' story feared: crossing a bridge at night willing to dive into cool water to rescue someone if that should prove necessary. Such involvement is difficult and it hurts! It doesn't necessarily need to be as heroic as diving off a bridge or building a bridge over a dangerous waterway either; we all have to claim and choose our involvements from our vantage points. However, the far-reaching, risk-taking, bridge-building love that extends beyond ourselves, even to our enemies—healing where there is suffering, bringing peace into situations of conflict—often works in quiet ways. Just as traffic on a bridge moves in two directions, when we reach out to others, others will reciprocate.

My father taught physics and astronomy at a community college for more than thirty years. When I was growing up, my father often showed us movies that he would bring home from his physics classes at school. A favorite my brothers and I often requested was a short movie documenting the collapse of the Tacoma Narrows Bridge in 1940. We would watch—eyes glued to the screen—as the bridge began to sway, cars scurried off to safety, and then pieces of the bridge started falling into the water. But as exciting as that was to watch, there was still magic to be done. As the film ended, my father would flip a switch and we would watch the bridge go back together again as he ran the film backward! Of course, in real life, the laws of physics followed their course and the bridge stayed collapsed. The moral of that story for the benefit of the physics students was that a structure cannot always bear the strain and stress that is placed upon it. I believe that the same holds true for those spiritual bridges that connect us all as God's creation on this planet. One bridge alone cannot bear the strain, so many bridges are required. I believe we are challenged to help build those bridges, each in our own ways, over the depressions and obstacles of our troubled world.

In my family, bridge-building and peacemaking began at home, not magically by flipping the switch on a projector, but through laughter and tears, bits and pieces of many languages, and a lot of hard work. This took place through reaching out to, and sometimes housing, international students who came to study in our community. Some relationships were easy to develop; others were painful and very difficult. In one particularly troublesome situation, my mother pointed out to my Greek brother, Christos, that he was free to criticize U.S. foreign policy if he chose, but he should remember that Henry Kissinger had never been a dinner guest at our house—and correspondingly, we had no personal influence on Kissinger's actions. In contrast, Christos showed up for meals three times a day and took full advantage of our hospitality while calling us "ugly Americans." In spite of the difficulties, the experience of having a brother from Greece, a sister from Brazil, and a brother from Nigeria taught me that it is a small world after all, but that world is indeed larger than the borders of a single state or country.

It is a difficult task to build bridges. Challenges can be met when people join together in community to help each other and work toward common goals. A church is one place where bridge-building can start, a place where people can share in the process of growing and learning together. I have collected notecards and quotations over the years and display them in my office to remind me of the challenges at hand. One quote from Sister Helen Kelley says:

> Choose life—only that and always.
> And at whatever risk.
> To let life leak out, to let it wear away
> by the mere passage of time,
> to withhold giving it and spreading it
> Is to choose nothing.[3]

A word of caution may be in order at this point. Choosing life should never be confused with saying "yes" to every situation that comes along. As we all know, there are many situations that are not so clear-cut that we can say one choice is all good and another is all bad. Even the most brilliant among us cannot predict the end results of our choices. Albert Einstein's revolutionary discovery that $E=mc^2$ produced results that contributed both to great good and to great evil. Shortly before his death, he is said to have written:

> I have found something else on the border area of mathematics and astronomy. And recently I destroyed it. To have committed one crime against humanity is quite enough for me. It will not happen a second time.[4]

Who knows the pride paid for that decision? Choosing life is not always easy.

Another saying goes like this: "If I'm not home accepting what I can't change, I'm probably out changing what I can't accept!"—a little twist to the "Prayer of Serenity." God is speaking to us today just as God spoke to the ancient Israelites. In fact, if Moses were here now, his challenge might be more urgent than it was centuries ago. We need to choose between life and death for our very survival—not just of one tribe or twelve, but of all the tribes on this planet!—depends on our ability to choose wisely. To choose death is to give in to fear and the forces of destruction at work in our world. To choose life is to take courage in both hands, to walk a path of construction drawing on God's strength and love as a resource, to go forth into the world willing not only to cross bridges, but to build them!

The choice is ours: Will we be members of a global demolition team or will we be architects and builders for God's kingdom? The bridges are waiting.

---

[1] Albert Camus, *The Fall*. Vintage Press, 1956, p. 15.

[2] *The New Merriam-Webster Pocket Dictionary*, Pocket Books, 1971.

[3] Card from The Pintery House, Conception Abbey.

[4] Quoted by a University of California–Berkeley student via electronic mail, Feb. 26, 1985. Exact source of Einstein's writings not located.

*O*ne flock, one shepherd

Joan B. Campbell

> *Joan Campbell*, coeditor of this book, is general
> secretary of the National Council of Churches. An
> ordained minister with standing in both the
> Christian Church (Disciples of Christ) and the
> American Baptist Church, she served previously as
> executive director of the U.S. office of the World
> Council of Churches. This sermon was preached at
> Riverside Church in New York.

John 10:11–18 and Psalm 23

Images of sheep and shepherds are very common in the scripture. And if you've ever been to Jerusalem or Bethlehem, Galilee or Nazareth, you would have no trouble understanding why. The scene even today is for the most part a pastoral one. It is not uncommon to see small gatherings of sheep with a shepherd poking and prodding them over the rough hillsides. How reminiscent it is of the well-known song, "David, Little Shepherd Boy."

But for most of us today, coming from cities, suburbs, or small towns, these agrarian images seem long ago and far away. Now I searched my mind for an image that would speak more clearly to us. And then one day, as luck would have it, I was walking down Riverside Drive and saw a group of small children—probably around two and a half to three and a half years old. And they were laughing and talking in the high, animated voices so characteristic of young children. Some, of course, were running—dangerously close to the street—and the teachers would prod and poke them back to safety, admonishing them to take care; occasionally hugging and kissing the hesitant, more fearful ones, calling their little lambs by name; and constantly and forever counting heads to make sure that not one was lost or forgotten.

Do you suppose that day-care workers might possibly be our equivalent of the Middle Eastern shepherd or shepherdess? The role that these day-care workers play is vital to the development of young children. In fact, we entrust to them our most precious possessions. We appreciate what they do. At least we say that we do. But like the shepherds of old, they are considered necessary but not terribly important in the world's terms—not powerful like a general or a corporation president, or maybe even a big steeple preacher. They surely are not our heroes or heroines. Maybe they're not even our role models, yet it was with the shepherds that Jesus chose to identify.

You have to use a little imagination when you read the scripture. Otherwise, it's just so many ancient words. And that is a little dangerous sometimes because you have to make some guesses, but I think the guesses help us understand. And I'm guessing that Jesus thought about the status of shepherds and, in fact, chose that he would identify with them. It wasn't an accident. For is not this Jesus, who says to us, "I am the good shepherd," the same Jesus who was led by the Spirit into the wilderness, into the desert, and there for forty days and forty nights was tempted by the devil himself? (Have you ever noticed how we don't ever try to change that gender language?) The desert experience, in the biblical understanding, was an encounter with illusions, with idolatries, and temptations. This Jesus, who chose to be remembered by us as a shepherd, was offered all the kingdoms of the world. This was his chance to be ruler of all he surveyed, to exchange a cross for a crown. He could have been the most powerful man in the world, with large armies to guarantee security, with wealth and recognition, with adulation and influence.

We have to believe that Jesus, the man, really wrestled with that temptation. Here again I invite you to use your imagination, picturing him there in the desert for forty days and forty nights. Because, you see, if he didn't really wrestle with the temptation, then there's really no purpose in the story being told. But he walked away from that temptation and he said, "I will worship God. Only God. And I will serve that God." He came out of the desert, not proudly claiming victory but with humility and with a passionate love of all God's people. Then he stood in the synagogue, and he defined his ministry in those ancient words from Isaiah as Luke records them: "The Spirit of the Lord is upon me, because he has anointed me to bring good news to the poor. He has sent me to proclaim release to the captives and recovery of sight to the blind, to let the oppressed go free, to proclaim the year of the Lord's favor" (Luke 4:18).

So the desert experience helped to define Jesus' ministry. His statement in the synagogue became the alternative to the illusions of the desert. A choice had been set before him. He didn't choose the death of unbridled power; he rather chose life—abundant, full, and free. But the very day, my friends, that he made that choice was the day that he became suspect. For how was the world to understand one who made such an unlikely, even a foolish, choice?

Choices have been set before us, individually and as a people, from that day to this. Not so very long ago now, we as a nation made a choice and our choice was to go to war. For many it seemed a triumph of military technology. For others it was a victory sufficient to reinstate our national honor and to claim leadership for America in this unique emerging period of world history. But all of us, whatever side of that issue we took, now face the task of serious reflection. This is a time to reflect on our national purpose, on our identity, and, most surely, on our Christian responsibility. Amidst the flurry of flags and yellow ribbons, we as Christians try to make sense of it all. One thing we know for certain: Desert storms create an illusion of strength. They blind us to history. They obscure the truth of the present, and they blur our vision of the future that God intends for God's people. We watch the nightly news and our senses become dulled. We see before our eyes a depth of human suffering that by its very magnitude is virtually incomprehensible. And yet the Good Shepherd calls to us from the ages and asks, "Do you love me? Feed my sheep. Do you love me? Tend my lambs."

This was a war that many of us thought could have been avoided. We took this position not because it was a politically correct position, but because we believe that war represents a failure for the human spirit. We feared that violence would beget violence, that the military solution to human conflict would only create more pain and more suffering. And so it has come to pass. People who neither benefited from this war nor wanted it are now its victims. Babies whose first breath has been drawn lose their lives before they ever have a chance to find them. The faces of young mothers whose milk has dried up stare at us from our screens, and the horror of the holocaust is etched in their hollow faces. Never has there been a war without casualties, and this one is no exception. To believe otherwise is an illusion.

We, as a nation, have opted to be ruler of the world and all that we survey. And, my friends, however benevolent and kind we might wish to be, the violence that surrounds us in our streets and in our homes and in our world is evidence that we have succumbed to the temptation of the desert. We face a deep and profound spiritual crisis.

The prayer lifted by thousands of Christians at the World Council of Churches Assembly in February, 1991, is exactly the right prayer for our day: "Come, Holy Spirit. Renew the whole creation." But when we call down that Spirit, we must be clear that we will be required to give up all of our illusions and our pretensions to prejudice and power, special status and prestige. There are no yellow ribbons or flags or marching bands for day-care workers or for shepherds. Almost unnoticed, they work diligently, with few resources, giving of themselves in order to nurture those in their care. Be very clear that for those of you who choose in this time to be life-givers—who make the choice for life in the middle of this seductive and acquisitive time—there will be misunderstanding and suspicion as to your motives. Some may even wonder about the sanity about such a decision. But if the church is to give leadership at such a time as this, perhaps it is the day-care model, the shepherd model, that serves us well—the shepherd who, you remember, says that he will lay down his life for his flock.

Philip Potter, the former general secretary of the World Council of Churches, when attending this past assembly of the World Council, was asked to define the characteristics that a church leader must possess in order to help others deal with these serious times in which we find ourselves. Philip drew himself to his full six-foot-three-inch frame and spoke to us in his deep voice. (His voice alone made you think something profound was to be forthcoming; there is a certain advantage to having a deep voice and being six-foot-three.) He looked at the group and said solemnly, "If you are to be a leader in this time, you must have a screw loose, you must have a death wish, and you must have a sense of humor." Well, that was not exactly what the waiting crowd had expected, and you could see them collectively draw a startled breath. With that half smile of his, Philip looked around and said, "Perhaps I should exegete the text."

"To have a screw loose," he said, "is to be open to the movement of the Spirit in your life—not to have life so carefully planned that the Spirit can't gain access. To have a death wish is to be clear that the choice to be a shepherd is to reject the crown for the cross. And to have a sense of humor is an absolute necessity to ward off the devil, for the devil never laughs." This, my friends, would certainly be a new set of criteria for search committees trying to measure church leadership. One can only wonder with amusement what it would mean for the church if these criteria were taken seriously. I would venture to say the cast of characters would change rather dramatically. But, you see, the church also has its temptations and its illusions. And day-care workers and shepherds are in short supply.

One of the great illusions is that we believe that we can attest to God's love amid our foolish divisions and our carefully drawn denominational differences. The spiritual crisis that we face in this nation demands that we respond to Jesus' prayers that we "be one...so that the world may believe" (John 17:21). We don't need to worry. We won't lose our identity. We won't somehow lose our sense of who we are if we risk being one. We are each unique and distinctive in God's eyes. God knows us and claims each one of us as God's own. The text for this morning makes it very clear that it is not the responsibility of the sheep to divide themselves into different flocks. It is only for the sheep to know the voice and the call of God; it is up to the shepherd to define who is part of the flock. Here the text is most instructive. Following the statement, "I lay down my life for the sheep," the text says, "I have other sheep that do not belong to this fold. I must bring them also, and they will listen to my voice. So there will be one flock, one shepherd" (John 10:15–16). And that is the most freeing and liberating reality that we could possibly be given. Think of the time and energy and pain and suffering that has gone into humanity's attempt to define who is in which fold and who is not, who is a member of the flock and who is clearly on the outside.

We have separated people by race, by gender, by class, by sexual preference, by denomination, by national identity. All of these are feeble and faithless attempts to define the flock. War and violence have been justified to protect the divisions that we have drawn, carefully defining who is friend and who is enemy. But we are told that there is one shepherd and so there is only one flock. That that flock is worldwide, and the shepherd calls us to feed, house, clothe, free, and nurture all in that flock, beyond boundaries and accidents of birth. This is the root of a world made new. This is the new world order. This is the way to peace. The question for our day is not, "Can we identify to which flock we belong?" The question for our day is, "Can we hear the shepherd's voice, and are we prepared to respond to the call?"

Sometimes words are just words. And sometimes it's not easy to internalize the meaning of those words for our lives. But every now and then, the truth is illumined for us by an incident that shatters our darkness and opens new understandings and possibilities. Such was the case for those of us who were privileged to participate in the Seventh Assembly of the World Council of Churches in Canberra, Australia, an assembly that took place during the war in the Gulf and that was affected by that war in profound ways.

Four thousand people from all over the world, both Christians and non-Christians, attended the assembly. I would venture to say that there is not a single person who has ever experienced a World Council assembly who will forget the first time that they saw God's people, speaking many languages, all colors, all varieties of dress, people whose governments are at war with one another, coming together—in this case in the gathering place called Canberra to pray together, "Come Holy Spirit. Renew the Whole Creation."

But the moment I'll never forget was the all-night prayer vigil for peace. Throughout the night, people from all around the world came together. All night there were people there from the countries of the Coalition Forces—French and British Christians, Egyptian Coptic Christians, the Syrian Orthodox—and there were Jordanians, Palestinians, and Iraqis. And we prayed side by side to the God of us all. We prayed for peace. There was Jean Zaru from the West Bank, a grandmother who had left home before the war and couldn't get back, and had no word of how her family was faring. And there was the rabbi who was there as a guest, the rabbi from Israel who electrified the assembly when he asked a simple question: "How do you think the Israelis feel—these people whose families died in gas chambers—when they are asked to put gas masks on their children?" And there was the Egyptian priest who had lost two brothers in another war in the Sinai.

Together, we heard from the preacher for this event, a preacher from the Universal Fellowship of Metropolitan Community Churches here in the United States. She had prepared a meditation on the meaning of oil, the way in which oil had sent us to battle, and the way in which oil was used in the Bible—oil for anointing and the oil of gladness. At the close of the vigil, those of us who were presiding were given a small bowl of oil from which to anoint the people who streamed forward. The choir sang very softly, "There is a balm in Gilead to save a sin sick soul." And the people came and they came, and it was a rich and powerful moment, but especially so when a young Native American by the name of Tolly Estes, who lives on a reservation here in the United States, came before me. He had tears in his eyes as he broke down and said, "Please pray for my brother. He is even this day in the ground forces in the Gulf." Right behind him in line was the Bishop of Baghdad and all Iraq. And I simply turned to the bishop and I gave him my container of oil. There they stood, and they anointed one another. Tears gave way to joy and in that special and blessed moment, the miracle of real peace—the peace that passes all understanding, peace way beyond cease-fires—seemed possible. For one brief shining moment, the barriers were down and we were one flock, and in our midst was the Spirit sent to us by the Shepherd who died that we all might have life abundant, full, and free. As the dawn broke, we each said in our own language that ancient and familiar psalm: The Lord, none other than the Lord is my Shepherd. I shall not want. He restores my soul. Even though I walk through the darkest valley, the Shepherd is with us. A table is prepared before me in the presence of my enemies. My head is anointed with oil, my cup overflows. Surely goodness and mercy shall follow us all the days of my life and I shall dwell in the house of the Lord forever.

Let the church say Amen.

*I*n search of a blessing

Jane McAvoy

Jane McAvoy is assistant professor of religion
at Hiram College. She is a graduate of Lexington
Theological Seminary, with a Ph.D. in theology
from the University of Chicago. This sermon was
prepared for an ecumenical service in South Bend,
Indiana, that sought to address the abortion
controversy through the telling of stories
of women who had illegal abortions in
the United States prior to 1973.

Psalm 22 and Psalm 23[1]

Why are you here? Have you been asking yourself that
question for the last few minutes as you have listened to stories
of women who made hard choices, endured suffering, even
risked death? Why did you choose to be reminded of their lives?
Why should you care?

I have been asking myself these questions ever since I was
asked to speak today. For me, the short answer is that I am here
because I was asked to be here by friends. These friends have
no idea whether I am pro-choice or pro-life. They are friends
with whom I have never attended a political rally, but with
whom I have a relationship that is one of caring and sharing. My
friends have a hunch that I would care for these women who we
commemorate today as I care for them. They assume that I
would search for a way to hear and understand their lives that
is not only political or moral, but faithful. They hope that I
would dare to search for God's word, even God's blessing. I
invite you to join me in this search.

But I must confess it is a hard, hard thing to do, a hard thing
to understand. Because we want to distance ourselves and to
distance God from stories of women who choose abortions. I find
myself wanting to add qualifiers, to ask, "Why?" Why didn't

they use birth control? Why didn't they give birth to their babies and have them adopted? Why weren't they more careful? Why didn't they just say no?

It is a great temptation to distance ourselves from these stories. We would not be like that, at least that's what we tell ourselves. After all, this is the end of the twentieth century when birth control is readily available, and women are fully able to make choices for themselves. If we are confronted with any facts to the contrary, we ignore them. We are like the doctor who ignored the plight of the married woman when he said, "Tell your husband to sleep on the roof...."[2]

Likewise, we are tempted to distance ourselves through the use of religious values. It is safe to say that for religious people, there is a universal belief in the sanctity of human life as a gift from God. In Jewish and Christian traditions, procreation has become the central symbol of divine benevolence. By invoking this principle of respect for human life, we can easily settle this moral dilemma. The debate stops. Abortion is forbidden.

The temptation to distance ourselves is powerful, because in the process we can remain assured that their stories will not become our stories. We remain pure, untouched by their pain, unstained by their blood. Of course, to do this we have to jeer at these women like the ugly mob jeered at the psalmist. We have to separate the world into self and other, the smart and the dumb, the good and the bad. In order to make sure we remain on the smart, good side, we have to judge them.

And we have to ground our distancing in a belief that God is distant from the plight of these women's lives. We cry, "Crawl to God to save you! See if God cares for worms!" Through our mocking, we imply God's estrangement and judgment on their lives. But even as we close our ears, their cries come through. "Do not stay aloof. Hurry, help me, God! Do not leave me as meat and drink for beasts of war. Pull me out of horror! Pull me free of carnage!"

What have we sacrificed in the effort to distance ourselves from these women's lives? We have labeled them worms, meat. And we have become "beasts of war, gods who nip at their bones and pick them clean." The shock of these words and the reality that women die from illegal abortions seeps into our hearts and minds. The stories are released as if they have escaped from Pandora's box. Once freed from the conspiracy of silence, they cannot be forgotten, no matter how hard we try to forget them.

So we are challenged to a new understanding. Challenged not only to become involved in the concrete reality of women's lives but to hear them as God hears them. Challenged to try to understand that their story is our story.

To meet this challenge, we must understand ourselves as being related to these women as our sisters, our very selves. The psalm that I chose for today, Psalm 22, is a lament that involves God, the lamenter, and the lamenter's enemies. The assumption behind such laments is that we exist in community. Unlike the false separation of self and other that our distancing demands, a hearing involves an understanding of ourselves as social beings, existing in relation to others and to God. As Phyllis Trible reminds us, in the telling of such stories, we are one blood.[3]

Furthermore, we must understand God as the one who hears us into speech.[4] At first glance, our stories do not seem to say much at all about God. Only one woman whom we have heard from today even mentions a relationship with God. But the psalmist cries, "God has not despised or abhorred my affliction, but has heard my cries." We might wish for a God who rides in on a white horse and saves women from death, a God who will save our society from the reversal of Roe vs. Wade. But the reality is that God hears us, and then we must be moved to act and to speak. It doesn't seem like much, but we must realize that hearing is the necessary first step in overcoming the evils of distancing. As the 23rd Psalm proclaims, "You are with me in suffering, hard decisions, even death."

With this new understanding, we still ground our thoughts in a respect for the value of human life as a gift from God. It is a great mistake to believe that only those who distance themselves can call on religious traditions. We respect human life, and we realize its social dimensions. We honor life, and in the process of real decisions, we need other values as well to choose between two human lives. Religious traditions wrestle with these values, and no easy and absolute decisions emerge. We are challenged to enter into the tough, real, messy reality of procreative choice.

And if we dare, we are drawn into the reality of women's lives. Despair, fear, guilt, rage, relief—these were some of the emotions felt by the women we remember. The radical nature of women's actions speaks of their desperation and reveals the real character of our struggle. We have to admit that we do not live in a perfect world. Not all relationships are loving ones, and not all children are wanted or cared for. Even in our age, ignorance about the consequences of sexual actions still abounds. Women still are forced into involuntary sexual acts by strangers, friends, lovers, and husbands. More subtle is our double standard that produces contraceptives, but labels women who use them as loose and immoral. Their story is a part of the injustice and inequality that we all still face and suffer from, no matter how much we would like to forget.

So we can strive to listen and to understand. But this is not enough. For even as the psalm does not stop with lament but calls for the removal of suffering, so too we are called to the removal of women's suffering in the sharing of these life stories. Like the nurse who was moved to work for procreative choice in the wake of one woman's death from an illegal abortion, we are urged to make sure that never again will women have to face such choices.

We will do so strengthened by hope, for we remember that in the ancient myth, the only blessing that did not escape from Pandora's box was Hope. As the psalmist declares, "The earth remembers care. All races pray for it. The poor shall eat their fill. Oppression will be ruled out."

We have hope too. Hope that respect for all human life regardless of sex, or class, or race will one day prevail. Hope that women will receive equal respect and will be understood as more than sexual objects. Hope that men will assume equal responsibility of the care and nurture of children and will be understood as more than sexual exploiters. Hope that every child will be a fully valued member of society and will be loved.

In telling and hearing, we seek to commemorate; in hoping and working toward the future, we find our blessing. So may we echo the psalmist's hope: "May our souls live, and may our futures proclaim you as the God who makes us whole."

------

[1] The version of these two psalms read at this service is by Francis Sullivan, *Lyric Psalms: Half a Psalter* (National Association of Pastoral Musicians, 1983). Quotations throughout this sermon are taken from that source.

[2] This and other references to women's stories are from accounts of women who have had illegal abortions in the United States. These stories had been read earlier in the service. This quote refers to the account of a woman who pleaded with her doctor to help her prevent further pregnancies because she was afraid she was not physically able to survive another pregnancy.

[3] Phyllis Trible, *Texts of Terror: Literary-Feminist Readings of Biblical Narratives*. Fortress Press, 1984.

[4] The idea of God hearing us into speech is suggested by Nelle Morton, *The Journey Is Home*. Beacon Press, 1985.

*E*mbracing sick foreigners (without condescension)

Drea Walker

Drea Walker is the new pastor of First Christian Church in Globe, Arizona, having previously served on the staff of First Christian Church in Bartlesville, Oklahoma. She is a graduate of Stephen F. Austin State University and Brite Divinity School. Drea's sermon was one of a series she and her senior pastor preached on "People Jesus Couldn't Forget (Even Though We'd Like To)," and grew out of a deep personal need to reflect homiletically about AIDS and our attitudes toward those who suffer from it.

Luke 17:11–19

My family on my mother's side is not large, so we cherish everyone associated with us. One of those family members, a cousin by marriage, died a few months back. John Cole, my cousin, died from AIDS. He did not contract the disease accidently from a blood transfusion. He was not an IV drug abuser. John was homosexual. He didn't learn to be a homosexual. He maintained it was just something that he was. It made him different from the rest of us in the family. It made him foreign to us. And to live by that lifestyle, he went off to a foreign place, the homosexual community in San Francisco. I never understood John's sexuality. It was too strange to me. I didn't and don't see how a man can be sexually attracted to men, or a woman to women. I don't understand it. I don't think I ever will. It is too different, too foreign, too alien to my own way of life.

The issue of homosexuality seems to be everywhere lately. The TV news magazine *48 Hours* recently devoted a two-hour special to homosexual life in America, the civil rights struggle of homosexuals against discrimination, and the physical and verbal abuse they continue to endure. This past week, the American Council of Reform Jewish Rabbis voted to permit the ordination of homosexual rabbis with the Reform tradition. It

155

was not a unanimous vote. Many of those voting for the measure said they did so on civil rights grounds, saying that sexual orientation does not impair a person's intellect or spiritual commitment and thus should not be an impediment to religious vocation. Those voting against it cited ancient traditions, biblical passages, and laws against homosexuality, asking where do we draw the line on what is and is not acceptable sexual behavior?

I cite the debate within Judaism because it occurred this week. That same debate has gone on in all mainline Christian denominations, and it continues. The United Church of Christ, our partner denomination, is caught up in controversy over the recent admission of a mixed gay and straight congregation to the UCC in one region, and the question over the ordination of homosexuals to ministry. We Disciples have continued to by-step the issue when it has come up in our General Assembly by refusing to rule on the question.

I seriously doubt that there would be as much attention given to homosexuality today without the AIDS crisis. This past week's *Time* magazine has a story on AIDS. There's nothing new about that—it's become so common, we're almost immune to them. This one cited the changing demographics of AIDS, how the percentage of AIDS patients who are homosexual has gone down as the number of IV drug abusers and heterosexuals has increased. The *Time* article said, "No one can deny that AIDS victims deserve all the compassion and help society can muster. The latest statistics presented at the [6th International AIDS] conference show that the toll is still mounting and the end of the epidemic is nowhere in sight. At least 600,000 Americans are infected with the virus, more than 136,000 have become sick and some 83,000 have died." Those are conservative figures. Some estimates double each of those numbers. Yet more than 60 percent of AIDS sufferers are homosexual, so the epidemic remains very much a homosexual issue, forcing the rest of us to confront both homosexuality and AIDS at the same time.

Is a homosexual lifestyle wrong? I used to say yes, it is wrong, without any doubt. But I'm not sure about that anymore. When I first began to study psychology fourteen years ago, homosexuality was still listed in the American Psychiatric Association's Diagnostic and Statistical Manual as a sexual deviance. It no longer is. It was removed from that classification several years ago, for a variety reasons. It was not a medical condition—there is no physiological aberration that causes homosexuality. Yet it is not a learned condition either—I know of no case studies that prove a particular individual became homosexual because he or she was taught to be so. There is also no psychological test that reliably indicates homosexual tendencies in either men or women. So it doesn't show up on medical tests, it doesn't show up on learning histories, and it doesn't show up on psychological tests. It shows up only if a person of homosexual orientation so identifies himself or herself as homosexual. So the APA removed it from its list of mental disorders.

Deciding if something is wrong or right is a moral issue, and that is one concern of the church. But the church has a greater concern: deciding what is sin, what separates us from God. *Is* homosexuality a sin? Perhaps. Perhaps not. That's not a wimp answer—it is part of a larger answer about the nature of sin itself. I believe the teachings of Jesus, as Paul wrote, that we are all sinners. We have all fallen short of the glory of God. Jesus did not spend his ministry building up a list of sins from lesser to greater. He spent his time calling all people to repentance, striving against the condition of sin with a capital S—the condition of separation from God, from which we all suffer. Some people persist in the notion that homosexuals are greater sinners than others because they suffer AIDS. When some people asked Jesus one day if some Galileans Pilate had killed were worse sinners than other Galileans for suffering such a fate, Jesus replied no, and he said that if the questioners didn't repent, they too would perish. He added that the people who had died when the tower of Siloam fell on them were not worse sinners than others because of their misfortune, but that if his listeners did not repent, they too would perish (Luke 13:1–5).

Jesus always reserved his strongest condemnations not for foreigners, but for his own people, the Pharisees chief of all. Not because they were evil, but because they too often relied on their own righteousness, and relying on our righteousness is sinful. For Jesus, sin was sin. It didn't come in pieces. If he considered it a waste of time to divide sin into sins and weigh one sin against another, why then do we waste our time doing that? Any of us, heterosexual or homosexual or even nonsexual, can use our God-given sexuality in sinful ways. Why waste time pondering the sinfulness of homosexuality versus heterosexuality? Be assured: You are a sinner, I am a sinner, we are all sinners. And we all need to repent. Once we confess that, the particulars of our sins—small *s*—become of very little importance. None of us has the right to be condescending toward other sinners, no matter what their particular sin.

In Sunday school today we learned about some of the people Jesus healed. One day Jesus and his disciples were traveling along the border between Samaria and Galilee. They came upon a group of ten men who had leprosy. The men cried out, "Jesus, Master, have mercy on us!" He answered, "Go and show yourselves to the priests," and as they went, they were cleansed. One of the ten was a Samaritan, who, as a non-Jew, could not go to the priest. So he turned back to give thanks to God by thanking Jesus. Though he was an alien to Israel, a foreigner whom many devout people were convinced that God ignored, Jesus blessed him, saying that his faith had made him well.

In contrast to his other healings, of lepers and other illnesses, it is not reported that Jesus touched this man. Apparently he didn't need to. But when the case called for it, Jesus did not hesitate to touch a leper, or someone with a fever, or someone withered with disease or unclean with ulcers or hemorrhages. He touched them. And he healed them.

The last time I saw John Cole was at our cousin Beth's wedding, three years ago. Did I touch him? Yes, I did touch John. I gave him a hug, as I always did. He was sick then, and we knew what he was sick with and why. But he was still John. I confess that I hesitated. I'd believed that when the time came, I'd have no reservations about touching an AIDS patient. But faced with the reality, I hesitated, though I knew that I was in no danger. With my own cousin, I hesitated. May God forgive me my hesitation. But then I hugged him, without reservation, without condescension, one human being to another, one child of God to another.

In the gospels' many accounts of Jesus' acts of healing, Jesus does not distinguish between his own people and foreigners. True, he clearly said he came first to the lost sheep of the house of Israel. Yet his message and salvation were for all people, in the tradition and spirit of the prophets before him and in accord with the eternal will of God. This was the lesson Israel had lost clear sight of. The danger of looking only inward at our own home needs is still with us in the church. Jesus' words in Luke 4:25f. bear repeating: "But the truth is, there were many widows in Israel in the time of Elijah, when the heaven was shut up three years and six months, and there was a severe famine over all the land; yet Elijah was sent to none of them except to a widow at Zarephath in

Sidon. There were also many lepers in Israel in the time of the prophet Elisha, and none of them was cleansed except Naaman the Syrian." And the people of Nazareth rose up to throw Jesus out of town, furious that he would remind them so pointedly that God's will was not always synonymous with their own. I wonder, how often do we react the same way toward those who remind us that God loves not only those of us in the church?

What are we to do, faced with the ones treated as lepers in our time, those with AIDS? In the June 15 edition of the *National Christian Reporter* newspaper, the "Dear Deborah" column had a letter from a pair of sisters torn over the death of their brother to AIDS. They had told some of their friends what their brother died of, and their parents, in fury, stopped speaking to the sisters. The sisters wrote, "It is bad enough to lose our brother, but our parents, too? Is this the Christian way?" Is it? I don't think so. We who sit here, and in other churches, all share a name: Christian. We share a title: disciple. We are both family and followers of Jesus Christ. I was forced to face up to my decisions about AIDS victims and homosexuals because a member of my own family had the disease, and lived by that lifestyle. Each week in this church, we proclaim that we are all children of God together. In the tradition and teaching of our Lord and Savior, we proclaim that sinners are children who have become lost from the family, and God seeks to bring them back in love. No one is irredeemable. No one is excluded from the love of God.

When our Lord left and ascended into heaven, he left the church in our hands. If the world wants to see what Jesus is like, they look to us to see him. It would be nice if it were the other way around, with people looking to him to see us, but that's not the way it is. This is an awesome responsibility with which Jesus has saddled us. If we are to live up to it, we must act as he acted, do as he did, speak as he spoke, love as he loved. To do this, we must touch the sick, even those who are foreign to us. We must embrace those foreigners—not wait for them to become like us first and then embrace them, but embrace them while they are still foreigners, without hesitation, without qualifications, and without condescension. We must not let their behavior determine our actions. Only Jesus' behavior should determine our actions. For it is to him that we will one day answer for what we have done, or failed to do, in his name.

John Cole made his peace with God before he died. He had been raised in a staunch Baptist Church in Texas, and grew up hearing that God is love, that salvation is open to all who ask for mercy, and that once you commit yourself into God's hands, God will never forsake nor forget you. John believed that. He did not believe that his way of sharing love was less than any other way. He gave the last years of his life in love, helping others who were ill with AIDS in spite of his own suffering, serving on the mayor's task force on AIDS, speaking out for research and care for other sufferers, and telling his own story, as I tell you his story now. He did not believe God would condemn him for his love. It is not for me, nor you, nor anyone else to condemn him, nor to decide his final fate, however alien his life was to ours. John committed himself into the hands of God. May we too show the faith of this "foreigner" and commit ourselves to God. May we, like Jesus, embrace the foreign ones among us, in his name, and by his grace.

On the edges of terror/on the edges of hope

Ola Irene Harrison

Ola Irene "Cricket" Harrison is associate
minister for Christian development at Downey
Memorial Christian Church in Downey, California,
and a doctoral student in theology and religious
education at the School of Theology at Claremont.
She is a graduate of Brite Divinity School. An
educator, musician, and poet, Cricket sees the line
between poetry and preaching as very thin and
often crafts her sermons in poetic form. This
sermon originated as a Maundy Thursday
communion meditation.

Mark 14:22–31, 66–72

One dark night late in 1982
I was driving between Fort Stockton and Sanderson, Texas
That's a long sixty-five miles on the best of nights
But I was driving back after Thanksgiving break
Back to teaching
Back to real life
And I was tired

Suddenly I saw it in the lane ahead of me
Unavoidable
The unmistakable stripe glistening white in the headlights
I looked to the left
I could swerve out of the way...
No luck
An oil truck was bearing down
I wouldn't have time to clear the lane

I looked to the right
No luck there either
Three deer stood poised on the edge of the ditch
Hitting them would be worse than hitting
The malodorous rodent ahead of me

161

Sometimes the best of our choices is a bad one
This was one of those times

I hit the skunk at 60-plus miles per hour

I paid dearly for that decision for weeks afterward
I felt an instant allergic reaction
That deepened into a full-blown lung infection
Over the next several days
Not to mention the tell-tale perfume in my car
For weeks

I had no other choice that night
I had done the only thing
        at least the best
                the most prudent thing possible
But even the best I could do was bad
Even the best
I could do was
Bad

The fourteenth chapter of Mark
Can be seen
As a tapestry
Woven out of persons' dark choices
Colors are muddy
Dull
Unclear
Images are disturbing and painful
Mark describes in stark detail
A night
When good and evil
Clash
Only to have evil
Take the upper hand
A night
When the shadows of human sinfulness
Lengthen
And deepen
To the point that they seem
Impenetrable

Preparing for this sermon
I ran through my mental catalog of sermons
I've heard (or preached) about Peter
                  some good
                  some not-so-good
                  some plain silly
                  some just wrong
Lots of sermons about Peter as HERO OF THE FAITH
                  SAINT OF THE CHURCH
Others about him as sniveling worm
                coward worse than all other cowards
(Poor, poor Jesus—just look at that awful Peter)
Few
At least in my memory
About Peter as human being

Painful as it is
We have to read this part of Peter's story
It is not enough to skip this text
Rush to Acts
Hold up Peter as a model preacher
But
Not enough to hold him as pariah
Untouchable
Scapegoat for our collective cowardice
We have to hear this part of Peter's story
Because it is our story as well

Peter is not even the protagonist in this drama
He plays his poignant scenes
On the edges of the crowd
As Jesus is hauled before the council
Then the High Priest
Peter followed at a distance
        not close enough to help
        not close enough to offer a word of comfort
        but close enough to watch
            close enough to wait

Across the centuries
We can hear his anguished rationalizations
"I couldn't have gotten too close
They would have had me too!"

Nilos Kazantzakis has Peter whining
"I'd do it because I love him...but the crowd would
Make mincemeat out of me!" *(The Last Temptation of Christ)*

If Peter was to step forward now
His life would be
Forfeit
So he waited
                waited in the shadows

I think one of the reasons this story cuts us so deeply
Is because Peter is altogether too
Touchable
Too easily understood
My own protests
So often uttered
"I wouldn't deny him! I'd be strong!"
Eerily echo Peter's words

"Even if they all forsake you, I will not deny you!"

And Christ's words haunt us still
"Before the cock crows twice,
You will deny me
Three times"

I cannot rail against Peter
My courage has holes in it too

Creeping into the light
On the edge of the courtyard
Peter was taking his first feeble steps of discipleship
While the gospel writer does not tell us
Peter's thoughts
It seems likely the turmoil of the evening
All the earlier events would weigh heavily upon his mind

Sitting at the table
Jesus' sad strange words
Horror
        Disbelief
                Anger
                    Confusion
As Judas was known as a traitor

The embarrassment of being caught
Napping in the garden
While his friend
His teacher
Struggled to pray
The ever-present danger of being discovered himself

Now
Cowering in fear
Trapped between
The demands of loyalty
And
The drives of self-preservation
He can't take the risk of
Being labeled a troublemaker
Peter dare not let the crowd know
He was one of Jesus' followers

Mark leaves Peter in tears
Goes on to describe Jesus' trial before Pilate
But
Peter is left in tears...
Broken trust, perhaps?
Shattered dreams?
Misplaced faith?

There are no tears more bitter than those of hopelessness
Unless they are the tears of ruined self-expectations....

Peter could deny knowing the man Jesus
But he could not deny the claims
Laid upon him by that Life
And on that night
It was precisely those claims that he was unable to fulfill

Could this be why this story hurts so much?
Because we are confronted with our own
Inability to live up to the claims that
Jesus lays upon us?
Because we come face to face with our own
Fears of loving another
Of facing rejection?
Because we fear the depths of our own pain?

Could it be that this story is so hard to take
Because Peter drags us
Kicking and screaming into
The courtyard of our hearts
Where Christ stands on trial day after day?

Three boys stood trembling before the principal
At that point the teachers involved
And the principal had heard
At least three different stories
With multiple retractions and additions
Enough to keep an appeals court
Busy for a year
Finally one of the boys said
"What good does all this do now?
I've already lied to you
And to my mom
I've already ruined everything…"

"I've already ruined everything"

"I am ruined."

And somehow
As strange
As impossible
As it may seem

Those three words may contain the seeds of our
        transformation

Still
What have we to say to Peter
Clinging there
Broken in the doorway
What can we offer to him?

Perhaps we give him his own memory
That earlier in the evening
Jesus sat at table
Blessed
And broke the bread

Judas
    Peter
        and all the others
One would betray
One would deny
But Jesus shared a meal with them
A meal shared on a night
Filled with dark choices
        broken trust
A night filled with pain
Remember that, Peter
Help us to remember it as well

Help us to remember that
Christ knows us
Our weaknesses and betrayals are fully understood
        fully forgiven
We stand in company
With Peter and the disciples
At the table
We may choose to deny our relationship with Christ
But we cannot destroy it
The hands that were soon to know the prints of the nails
Reached out to Peter before the denial

The hands that carry the scars reach out to us now
At this table we find what Peter found
Unconditional acceptance
Fully known
Fully loved

It was shattered in a hundred pieces on the floor
Her mother's prized sugar bowl
Depression glass
Cobalt blue
Deep rich color in concentric rings
It was beautiful
And she loved it

She was just old enough to stay by herself
For ten minutes or so
Long enough for her mother to run to a neighbor's house
    on an errand

Long enough to climb up
Grab the beautiful thing
Only to have it slip from her chubby fingers
She cried
Knowing her mother's hurt and disappointment
Feeling the sense of broken trust
(Though she was too young to put that into words)
Clumsily
Quickly she swept up the pieces
Threw them away
Then went outside to hide
Long after that she heard her mother
And then saw her mother's sad face
In her mother's hand the knob off the lid of the broken bowl
(How had she found it?)
And then her mother's tired words
"What can you tell me about this?"

Childish confession poured out
Word upon word
Ending in
"I knew you would be mad so I hid out here
Before I ran away"

Mother and daughter both cried
Quietly the gift of forgiveness came
In her mother's words:

"There's nothing you can change
By hiding out here
All by yourself—
Why don't you come in to supper?"

Come in to supper....